I0462745

Reg's Practical Guide Series Presents:

Making Sense Of Downloading Pictures And Music To Your Computer

By Reginald T. Prior

Copyright © 2010 by Reginald T. Prior

Cover design by Reginald T. Prior
Book design by Reginald T. Prior

All rights reserved.

No part of this book may be reproduced in any form or by any electronic or mechanical means including information storage and retrieval systems, without permission in writing from the author. The only exception is by a reviewer, who may quote short excerpts in a review.

Reginald T. Prior

Visit http://www.rcsbooks.com or E-Mail me at reginaldprior@gmail.com

Printed in the United States of America

First Printing: March 2010

ISBN - 1453861343
EAN - 139781453861349

Trademarks And Copyrights

Trademarked and or copyrighted names appear throughout this book. Rather than list and name the entities, names or companies that own the trademark and or copyright or insert a trademark or copyright symbol for with every mention of the trademarked and or copyrighted name, The publisher and the author states that it is using the names for editorial purposes only and to benefit the trademark and or copyright owner, with no intentions of infringing on the trademark and or copyrights.

Warning and Disclaimer

Every effort has been made to make this book as complete and accurate as possible. No warranties are implied. The information provided is on a "as is" basis. The author and the publisher has no liability or responsibility to any individuals or entities with any respect to any loss or damages from the information provided in this book or from the use of the utilities CD or any programs on it.

Preface

There are many books on the market that teach people how to use their computers. But as I look through these books, I found that they teach some of the tasks about operating their computers, but miss a lot of critical things about fully utilizing their computers. Also I found with a lot of these books that they do not fully explain computer terminology at all in laymen's terms or teach people how to backup and restore their critical data (Documents, Pictures, etc) on their computers in case of a computer malfunction or viruses attacking their computer.

My aim of this book is to fill in these gaps in computer literacy that most books do not cover or spend sufficient time covering in common sense and in a way that is easily understood by everyone. As a computer technician for 12 years, I have come across many people that understand some things about computers, but want to have a better understanding about how they work and to fully utilize them in their everyday lives.

In this book, I will be covering how to effectively download and organize your digital photos and music files utilizing two programs, Windows Media Player and Google's Picasa photo management program.

You as the reader are the most important critics of this book. I value all of your feedback and suggestions that you may have for future books and other things that I can do to make these books better. You can e-mail me at reginaldprior@gmail.com and please include the book title, as well as your name and e-mail address. I will review your comments and suggestions and will keep these things in mind when I write future texts. Thank you in advance,

Reginald T. Prior

Acknowledgements

This book that you are reading right now takes a lot of time and sacrifice to put together. I would first and foremost thank God for giving me at the age of six the love of working on computers that still is as strong today as it was back then. I would like to thank my wife, Sharifa for being a trooper when I was spending many hours on my laptop putting this book together and also for being there to help me read my drafts to make sure that it would be understood.

Also I would like to thank my family and many friends that helped and supported me throughout the years on many other projects and being there for me in good times and bad. I hope that you all enjoy this book as much as I had putting it together.

Table Of Contents:

Before we go into learning how to operate Computers in general, I believe that before you can build knowledge in anything, we have to build your knowledge like a builder builds a house. First we have to have a solid foundation laid down before we can start building floors and rooms within the house. Fully understanding computer terminology and knowing what it means is like laying the foundation on the house.

In this section, I aim to translate what geeks talk about when we are talking about these parts and more on a computer. Decode the foreign language so to speak. This is not a full list of computer terminology, which would be a book by itself. But this is a list of the most common terminology used for talking about things with a computer. So with no further delays, lets get started laying the foundation to being confident to speak "Computer Language".

Computer Terminology

Hardware

Hardware is the actual pieces of the computer that you can see and touch. A computer monitor is considered hardware, a computer tower or laptop is actual hardware. Printers, scanners, mouse and keyboard are considered as hardware.

Software/Programs

Software is the programs on your computer or you can buy or install that does a specific task. For example, your word processor like Microsoft Word, Excel, and PowerPoint are programs designed to create documents, spreadsheets or presentations. Microsoft's Internet Explorer® web browser is a program designed to get onto and browse the Internet.

Note – You need hardware and software working together to make your computer work. Just having one without the other is like having a car with no gas in it.

Hard Drive/Hard Disk

The hard drive is an actual part inside the computer that information is saved to. We can refer the Hard drive (Usually the C: drive in the My Computer Section) as a file cabinet that everything is stored. Inside the file cabinet are files and folders that represent our things. We would organize our files in folders so that it would be easier to pull out the things we want to see. The same thing goes in computers.

Within our file cabinet, there is a folder called My Documents, My Pictures, My Music. Ideally we would create folders within these folders to identify what is inside them. There are removable or portable hard drives which you can plug into the computer and remove from the computer for additional storage, but I would only recommend these for backup purposes.

Ram/Memory

Memory could best be described as short-term storage of the computer. It is where information is stored for short periods of time. That is why it is very important to save your work constantly just in case of a glitch happening with the computer causing it to restart or freeze up because it is only there until the computer turns off, then it is gone forever. Of course the more you have of this, the better.

The way that a computer uses the hard disk and memory to operate together can best be described as this. We remember quickly what we had done yesterday, but if we are asked about things that happened last year, we would have to think harder (Referring to our brains "Hard Drive" to remember things that happened a while ago and recall it into memory) this is how basically how information is exchanged in the computer. The computer takes information from the Hard Drive and loads it into its memory so that it could be worked with or remembered quickly.

Mouse

The mouse is the hardware device that is connected to your computer that looks like a flattened egg that controls the cursor on the screen. You use this device by sliding it across a "Mouse pad" or any other surface on your desk or table. The mouse has 2 buttons for clicking to perform an action. You can either "Left Click" or you can "Right Click". A picture of a mouse with which buttons are the Left or Right Click is shown on below:

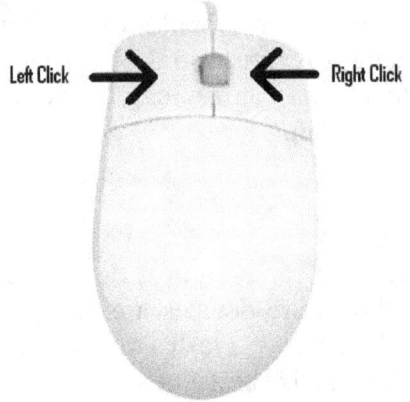

Cursor

A cursor is one of two things. A cursor can be an arrow or another shaped object that moves around the screen when you move your mouse around. It acts like a pointer on the screen so that you can perform an action by Left or Right Clicking your mouse. Also a cursor can be the blinking vertical line in programs such as word processors to indicate where you are typing.

Double and Single Clicking

A Double Click is an act where you press the left side of the mouse down quickly twice without moving the mouse at all. A single click is the act of pressing down the left side of the mouse once without moving the mouse at all.

Keyboard

Keyboards are hardware devices that have different letters on keys that allow you to type.

Printer

Printers are hardware devices that perform duplication or prints.

Scanner

A Scanner is a hardware device that is connected to your computer that allows you to import items into your computer such as pictures that you have or documents that you have to save to e-mail, duplicate or archive digitally.

Icon

Icons are small pictures on your screen that can represent many things. On your desktop (The main screen on the computer), Icons can represent the programs or software that are installed on your computer. You would left double-click the picture to start and work with that particular program. Throughout this book, you will see that Icons can represent things you can do within certain programs also. Like in a word document, you can have a menu with many icons on them that can represent sending something to the printer to print to saving among many other things.

USB Port

The USB Ports are ports where you can plug in various devices. It is a very versatile type of connection because many hardware devices are being made to use these ports from Printers and Scanners, Digital Cameras, Flash Drives and many more things. A picture showing what a USB Port looks like is shown below.

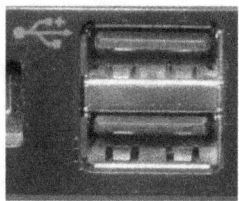

Flash/Jump Drives

Flash/Jump drives are one of many types of removable storage. These devices are plugged into one of the USB Ports. Files, Pictures and other things can be saved to this device. These are now being used in place of floppy disks. A picture of what a Flash/Jump drive looks like is shown below.

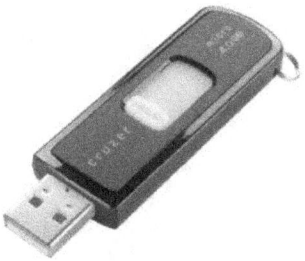

CPU/Processor

The CPU/Processor is the "Brain" of the computer. It actually is the part of the computer that does all of the thinking for the computer.

Gigabyte

Gigabyte is a unit of computer memory or data storage capacity equal to 1,024 megabytes. The term Gigabyte can refer to both computer Hard Drives and Computer Memory. You can tell the difference about which gigabyte it is by knowing that the computer memory is always referred by the smaller number and the computer hard drive space is referred to the larger number.

Like I had stated earlier in this chapter, these computer terms or definitions are not all of the terms we talk about when we geeks discuss computers. Not by a long shot. Most other terms are out of the scope of this particular book. But the above translations of the "Computer Lingo" are all of the terminologies that you need to know to effectively be knowledgeable and comfortable operating a computer. I hope that I did not put you to sleep with all of this computer terminology and their meanings. But it is necessary to be able to follow along with the rest of this book.

The next chapter of this book goes into the fun stuff. Getting into and actually working with your computer, which is the main reason why you purchased this book! With no further delays, let's proceed to using Picasa to download, scan and organize your digital photos.

Using Picasa To Download, Organize And Print Pictures

Over the past ten years or so, photography has taken a dramatic shift. That shift being the switch from film to digital. For decades, people have been taking pictures using film cameras. The process of getting pictures with film cameras was to take pictures until the film ran out, then taking the film to a photo developer to get the pictures. Then buying and installing a new film cartridge into your camera to take more pictures.

Most people were used to doing this. But with digital cameras, the process has dramatically changed. Digital cameras have memory cards instead of film that can be reused over and over again. Now you have two options of getting pictures from your digital camera.

One of your options is to take the memory card from your digital camera to the photo developer. Most of them now have digital processing machines that process your digital photos like your old film cartridges. The second option is to download the pictures from the memory card to your computer and print them out with your printer.

Many people have issues with the process of doing the latter. And I find that the photo programs that come with many digital cameras don't simplify that process. Not until Google released Picasa, their photo management program. Picasa is a very powerful but simple program. We will be going into detail about how to download your photos, step by step in the following sections.

Before we can work with Picasa, we have to make sure that it is installed on your computer first. To get Picasa, open up your web browser and in the address bar, single left click on it and erase everything that is there by pressing the backspace key on your keyboard. After you have done that, type in http://www.picasa.com and press the enter key on your keyboard. The Picasa website will come up as shown in the picture on the next page:

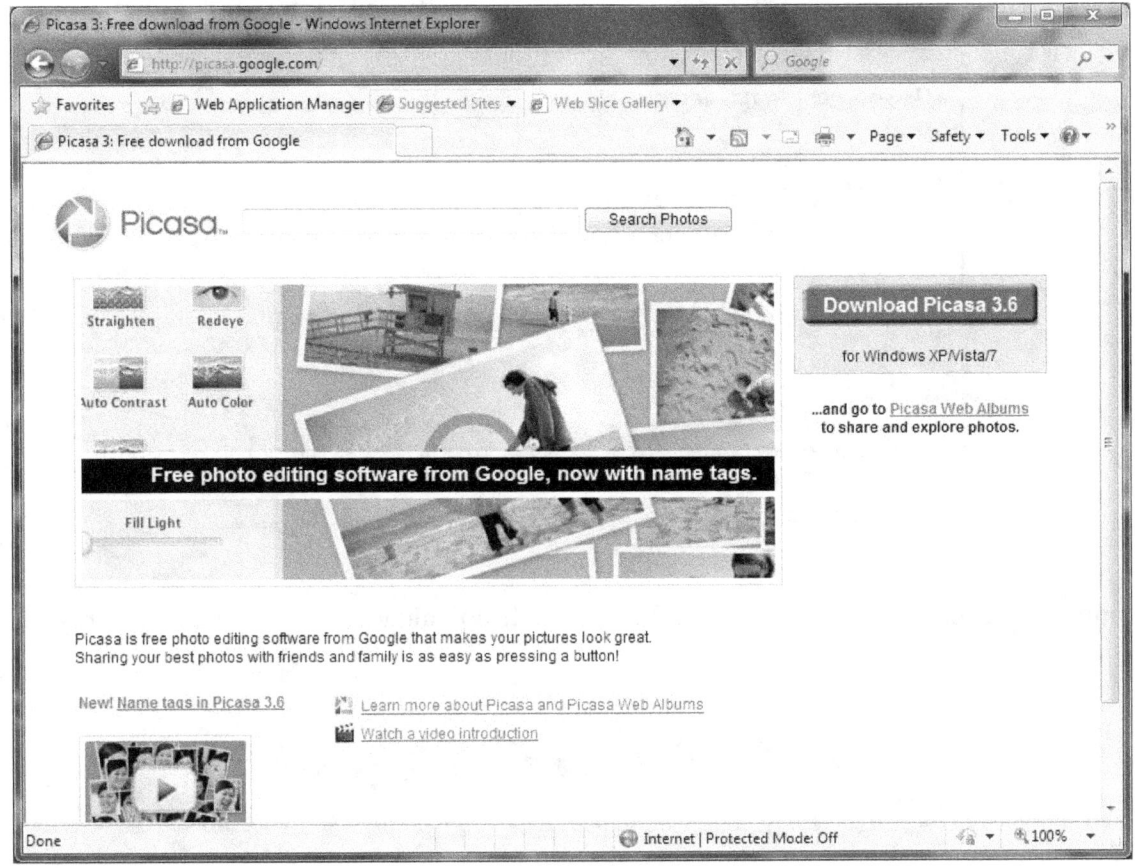

To download Picasa, move your mouse cursor to the "Download Picasa" link and single left click on it. If you are using Internet Explorer, A warning window will show up at the top of the webpage telling you that Internet Explorer has blocked you from downloading files to your computer and to click here for options. It looks like the picture shown below:

To help protect your security, Internet Explorer blocked this site from downloading files to your computer. Click here for options...   ✕

Move your mouse cursor to this window, single left click on it and another box will pop out. One of the options in that box will be "Download File". Single left click on that option. Internet Explorer will ask you what do you want to do with this download as shown in the picture on the next page:

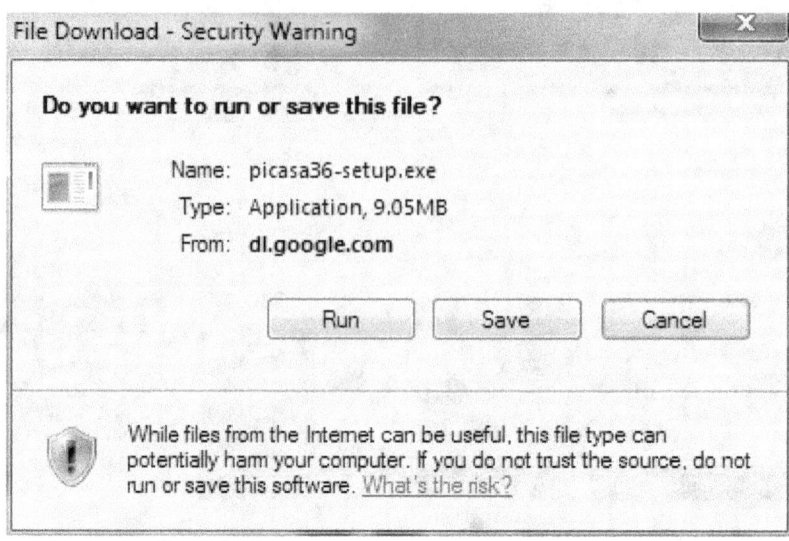

Single left click the "Run" button and Picasa will download and start installing on your computer.

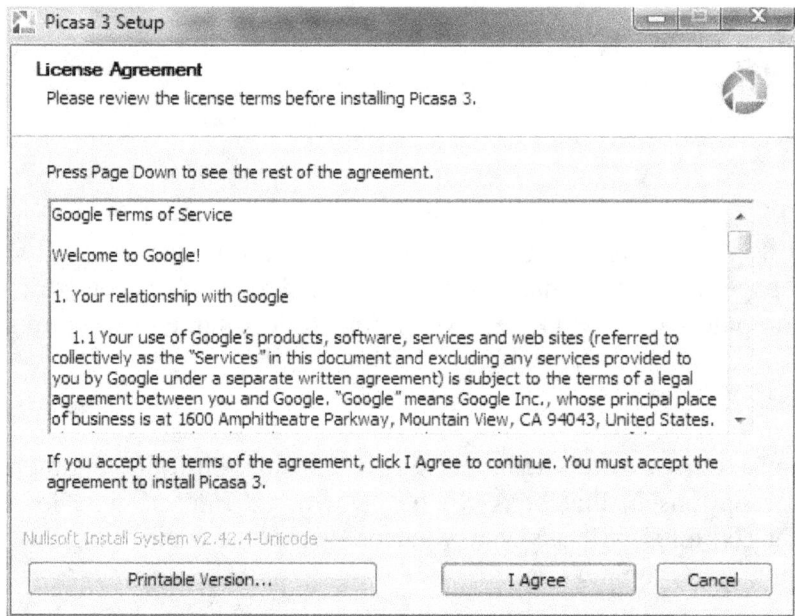

This is the first window in the Picasa installer. Before we can continue, we have to "Agree" with the Google license by single left clicking the "I Agree" button as shown in the picture above:

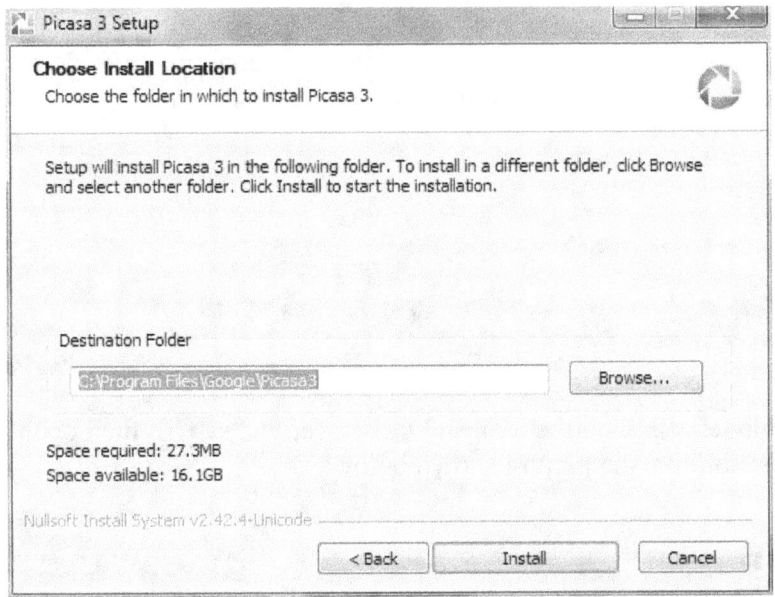

This is the second window in the Picasa installer. Single left click the "Install" button as shown in the picture above. Picasa will now install on your computer.

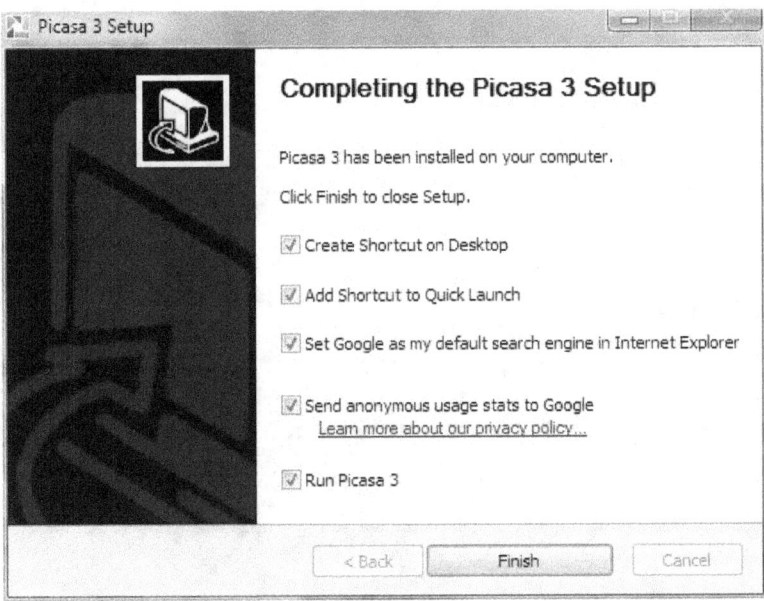

After Picasa successfully installs on your computer, the picture shown above is the final window in the Picasa install program telling you that Picasa has installed on your computer without any problems. Single left click the "Finish" button and you have installed Picasa on your computer.

After you have downloaded and installed Picasa onto your computer from http://www.picasa.com, the program will leave an icon on your desktop you would double left click on to open the program. The icon looks like this:

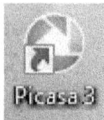

After you double left click on the icon shown above, Picasa will then open up to the main screen that will look like the picture shown below:

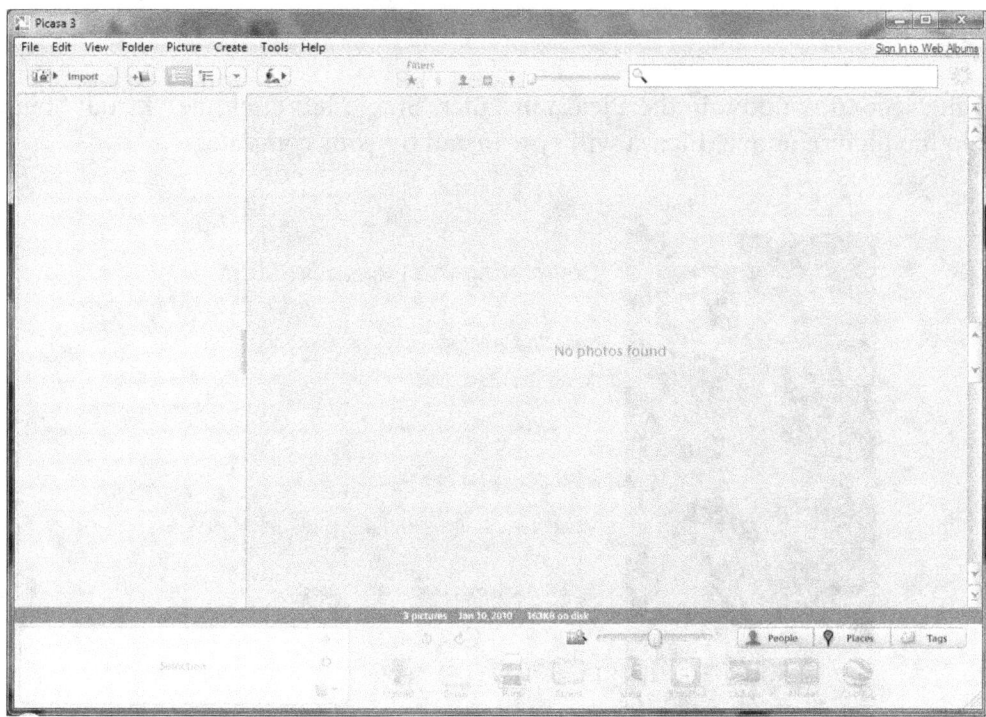

As you can see, Picasa is divided into several parts. We will go over each part in detail in the next section.

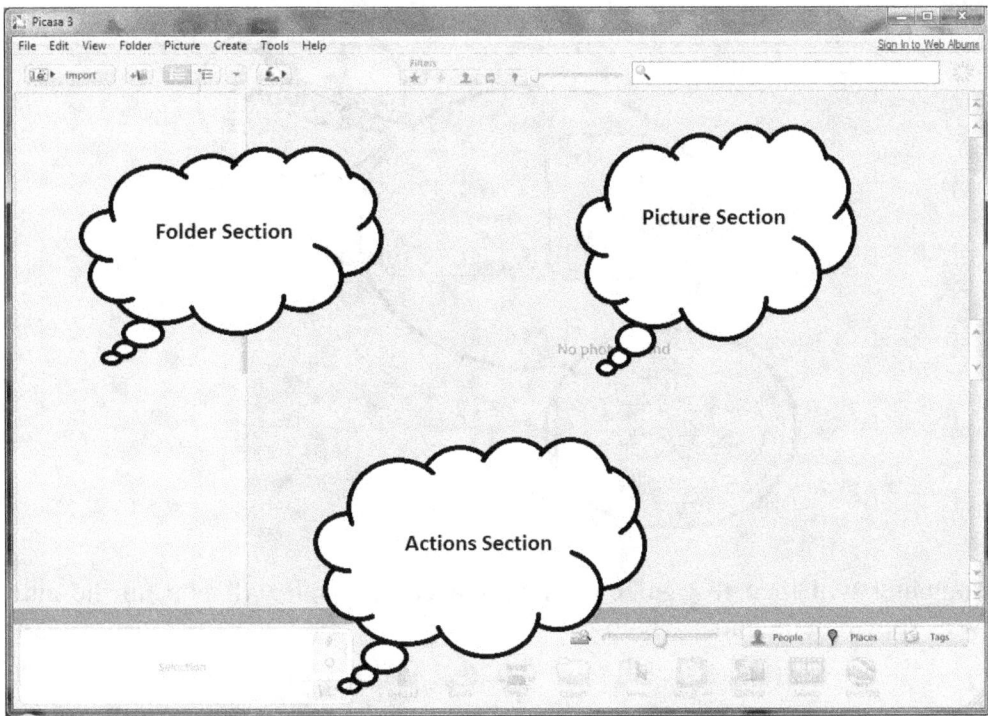

Picture Section - This is the section where previews of pictures will show up when you single left click on a folder in the folder section.

Folder Section – This is the section where you will organize your pictures into albums for easy and quick access.

Actions Section – This is the section where you would tell Picasa what you want to do with a picture or album you have selected.

Downloading Pictures From Your Digital Camera Into Picasa

Before we can work with pictures in Picasa, we have to download pictures from your digital camera into Picasa right? To download pictures to your computer, first connect the one end of the USB cable that came with your camera to the camera and the other end to a USB port on your computer as shown in the picture on the next page:

Note – After you connect your digital camera to your computer, check the viewer window on your digital camera. Some digital cameras require you to push a button on the camera to make the camera connect with your computer.

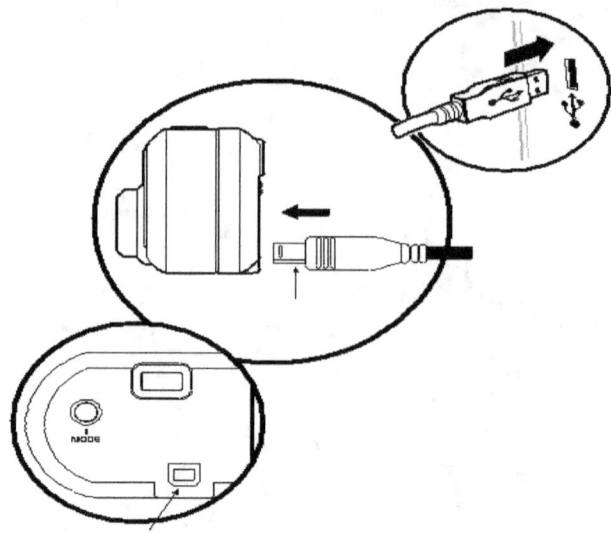

Your computer will then recognize your digital camera and will pop up the auto play window as shown in the picture below:

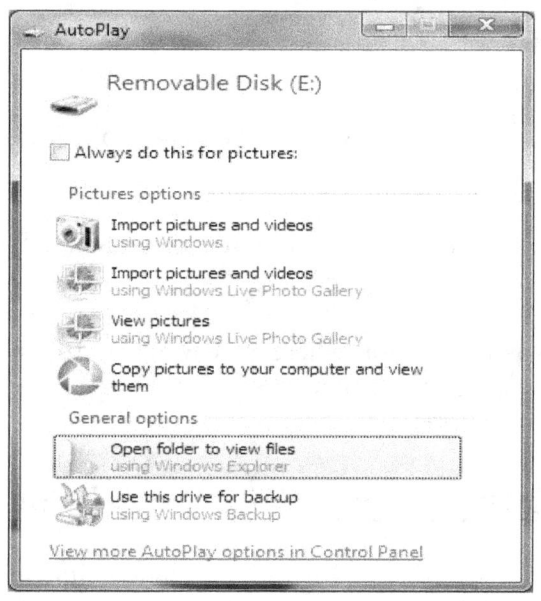

Single left click the "X" on the top right of this window and the window will close. Open up Picasa by double left clicking the Picasa icon on the desktop.

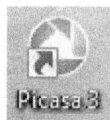

Picasa will open up to the main screen. To import pictures to your computer, single left click the "Import" button on the top left part of the main window. The button looks like this:

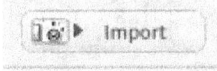

Picasa will connect to your camera and show the pictures that are on the camera as shown like the picture shown below:

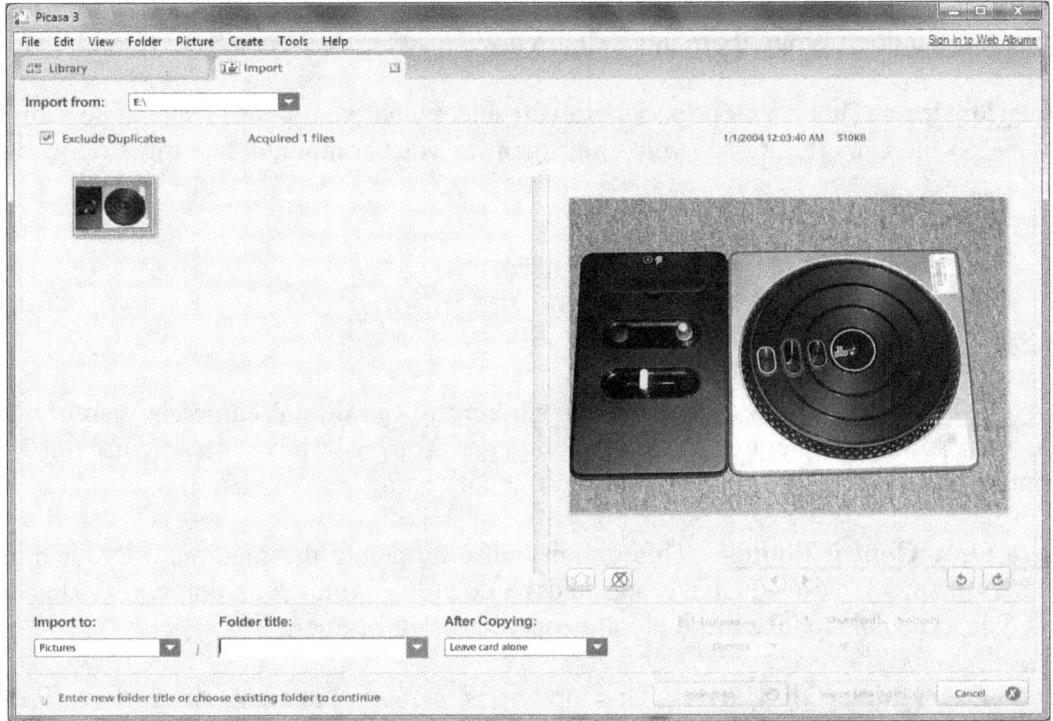

By default, Picasa is going to only have the first picture highlighted for downloading into your computer. To download more than the one picture that is highlighted, hold down the "Ctrl" key on your keyboard, then move your mouse and single left click on each picture you want to download to your computer.

At the bottom of this window, there are three options for importing your pictures as shown in the picture below:

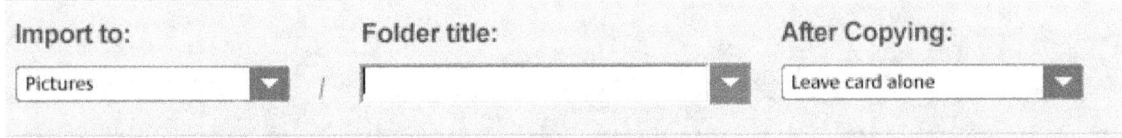

Import to, Folder title, and After Copying. We will go into more detail about what each option means next.

Import To - This is the option where you can select a specific folder where you want pictures downloaded into. Always leave this option to download to the "Pictures" folder. It will make it very simple to backup your computer.

Folder Title – This is the option where you can name a title for downloaded pictures. If these pictures were taken at a family reunion, I would name it for example "Family Reunion 2010" or something that would easily identify these pictures. Believe me, when you take a lot of pictures, it can easily become a nightmare trying to identify a group of pictures if you don't group them in an album now.

After Copying – This is an option where you select what you want Picasa to do with the pictures on the camera after downloading them to your computer. The three options are listed below:

After Copying Options:

Leave Card Alone – This option will do nothing to the digital camera's memory card after you download pictures to your computer. You will have the picture on your computer and also on your digital camera's memory card.

Delete Only Copied Photos - This option will only delete the pictures on your digital camera's memory card you have selected to download into your computer. This will allow you to be able to take more pictures on your digital camera.

Delete Everything On Card - This option is self explanatory. After downloading pictures to your computer, Picasa will delete every picture on the digital camera's memory card no matter if you selected it to download to your computer or not. Make sure that you really want everything deleted on the card before selecting this option!

After going through this section of the import menu, single left click the import button of your choice. If you only selected a few pictures, the single left click the "Import Selected" button. If you want to import every picture off the memory card into your computer, then single left click the "Import All" button. Your pictures will download to your computer. A picture of the import buttons are shown below:

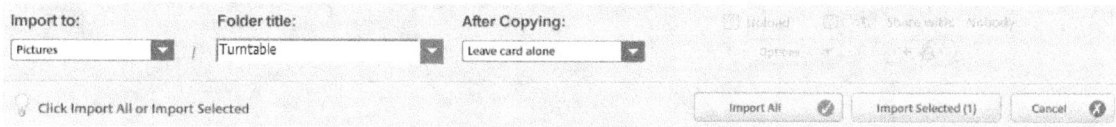

Scanning Photos From Your Scanner Using Picasa

Do you have photos in albums, wallets or other places you want to preserve or e-mail to others? To do this, you have to use a flatbed scanner or all in one printer that look like one of the pictures shown below.

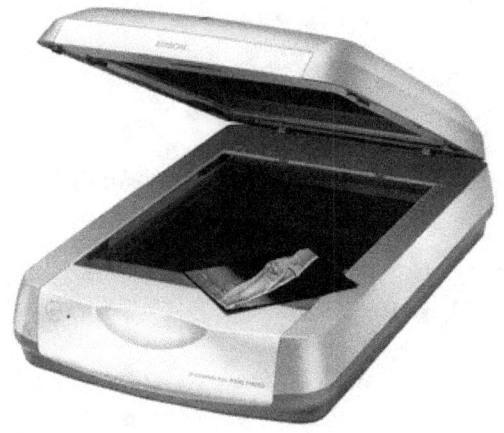

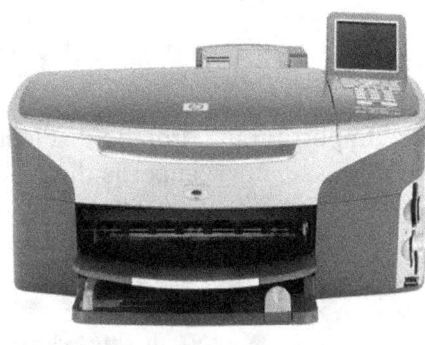

Flatbed Scanner   All-In-One Printer and Scanner

The first thing you would do is to turn on your scanner. Your computer will then recognize your scanner and pop up the auto play window as shown in the picture below:

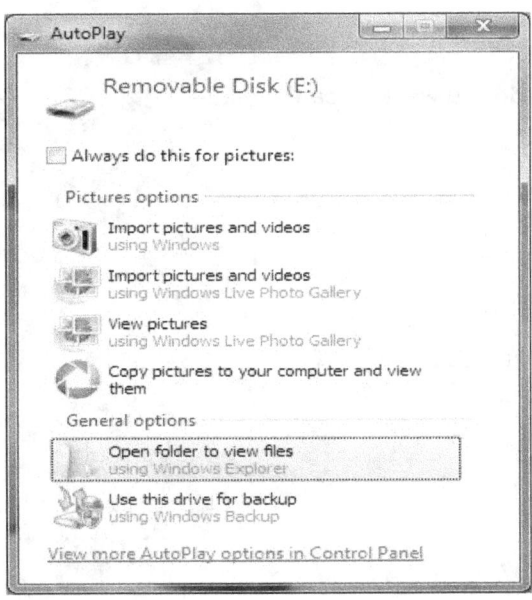

Single left click the "X" on the top right of this window and the window will close. Open up Picasa by double left clicking the Picasa icon on the desktop.

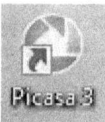

Picasa will open up to the main screen. To start importing pictures to your computer, single left click the "Import" button on the top left part of the main window. The button looks like this:

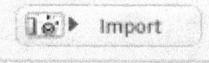

In The "Import From" drop box, select your scanner by single left clicking on it in the list. In this case, my scanner is the Kodak 5500.

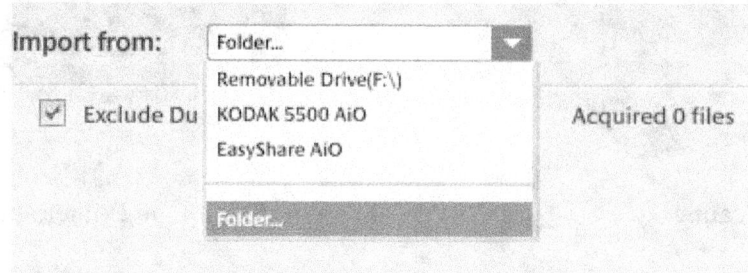

When you select your scanner, the Windows scanning program will come up as shown in the picture below. Place the picture you want to scan on the scanner flatbed.

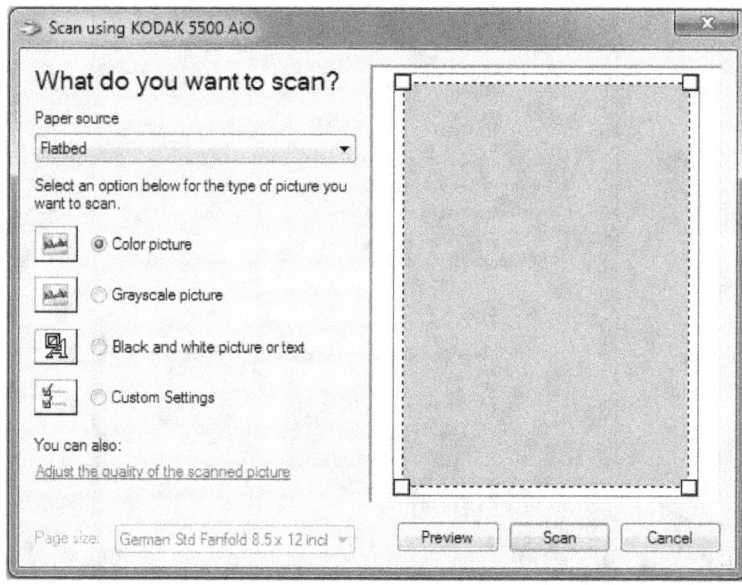

Single left click the "Preview" button in the windows scanning program. The program will do a preview scan and crop around the picture as shown in the picture on the next page:

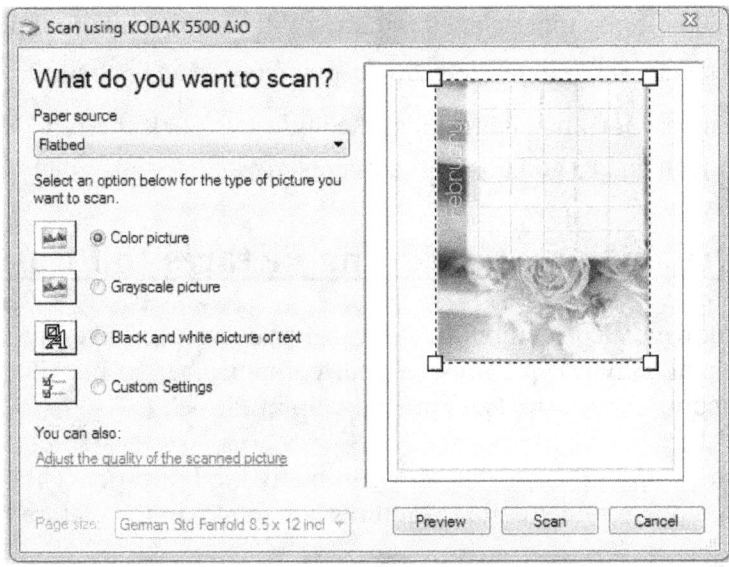

Single left click the "Scan" button to do the final scan. Your final scan will look like the picture shown below.

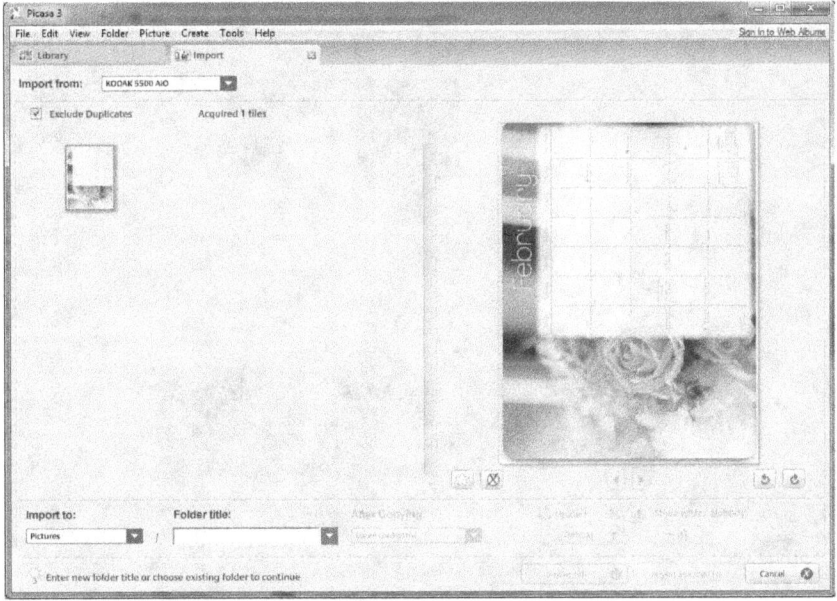

As you can see, the picture that has been scanned into the import menu in Picasa is vertical instead of horizontal like the original picture. To turn the picture around, Use the two buttons underneath the final scan to correctly orient the picture. The buttons look like the picture shown below:

After you correctly orient the scanned picture, Fill out the album information at the bottom of this menu and single left click the "Import All" button. You have now successfully scanned your photo into Picasa. Single left click the red "X" on the import tab to close this menu and to go back to the main screen.

Organizing And Editing Pictures In Picasa

After you have downloaded pictures into Picasa, you want to have an easy way to find them right? If you already had pictures on your computer before installing Picasa, Picasa will search your computer and make them show up in Picasa.

But when they show up in Picasa, they are not in any kind of order. They are all over the place. They come up in a folder called "Pictures" as shown in the picture below:

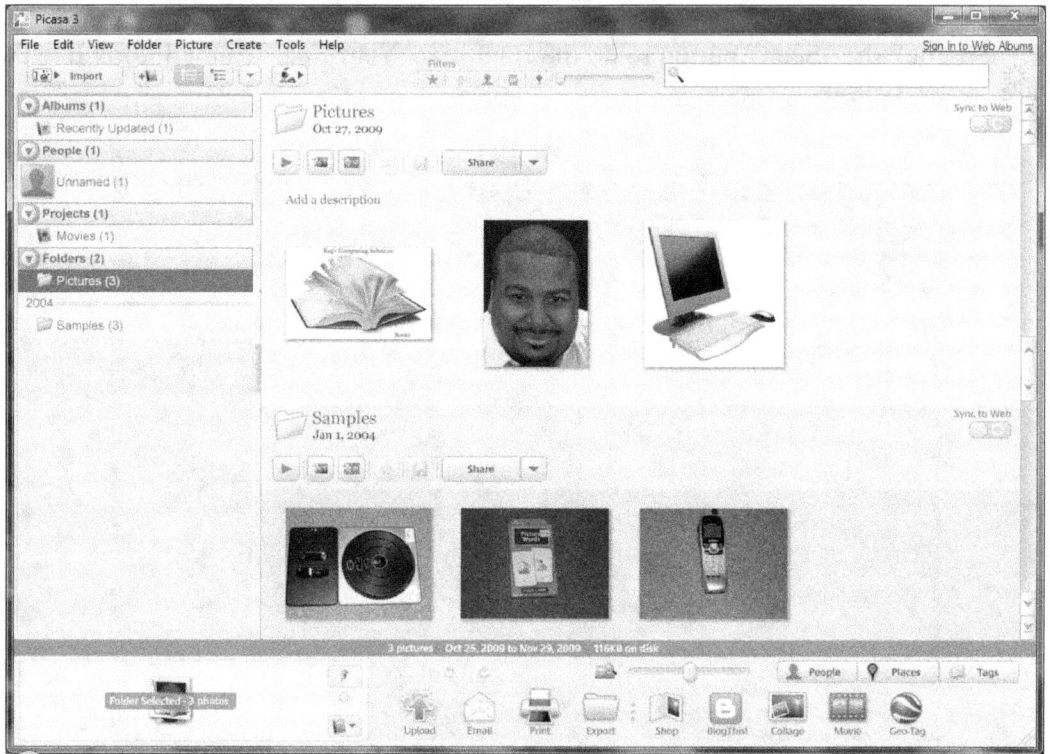

As you can see, each picture represents something different. One picture is the logo of Reg's Computing Solutions Books, Another picture is of me, and another picture is of a computer. We will organize pictures into separate albums so that in the future, you can easily identify them.

To create a new photo album to organize a group of pictures, on the main window next to the import button, there is the "Create A New Photo Album" button. The button looks like this:

Single left click on this button and the album properties window will pop up as shown in the picture below:

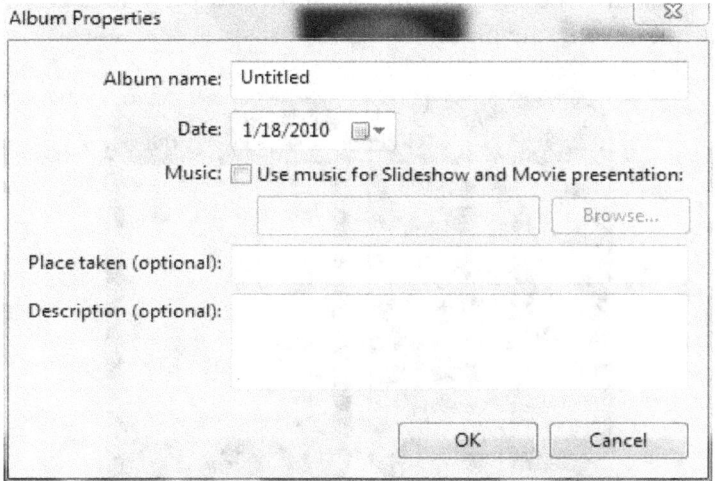

Type in a name for this album in the "Album Name" box, and select the date when you think that these groups of pictures were taken and single left click the "OK" button. Your new album will show up in the "Folder Section" under the albums section as shown in the picture below:

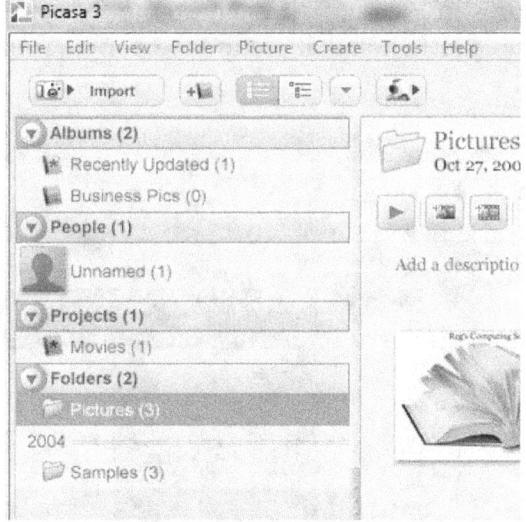

I have named this particular album in my example "Business Pics". I am about to move 2 pictures into this album. I am about to move the logo for Reg's Computing Solutions Books and also the picture of the computer into this album.

To move pictures into an album, simply hold the "Ctrl" key on your keyboard, then single left click the desired picture to move and hold the left mouse button down. Drag the picture to the album in the "Folder Section", and release the left mouse button to put them there. The pictures are now organized in the newly created album.

How To Crop Pictures In Picasa

What if you have taken a perfect picture of someone only to have something in the picture you rather not have in the picture at all?

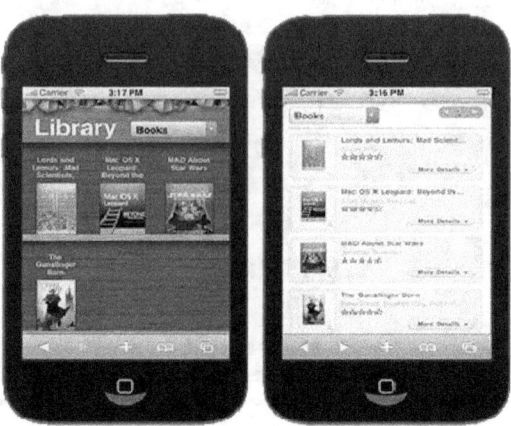

In the picture shown above, you see a picture of two IPhones. But what if I want to only have the IPhone on the right instead of both of them? Picasa allows you to crop out items in pictures. To crop pictures in Picasa, first open up the Picasa Program, find the picture you want to crop and double left click that picture to open it. Your screen should look like the picture shown below:

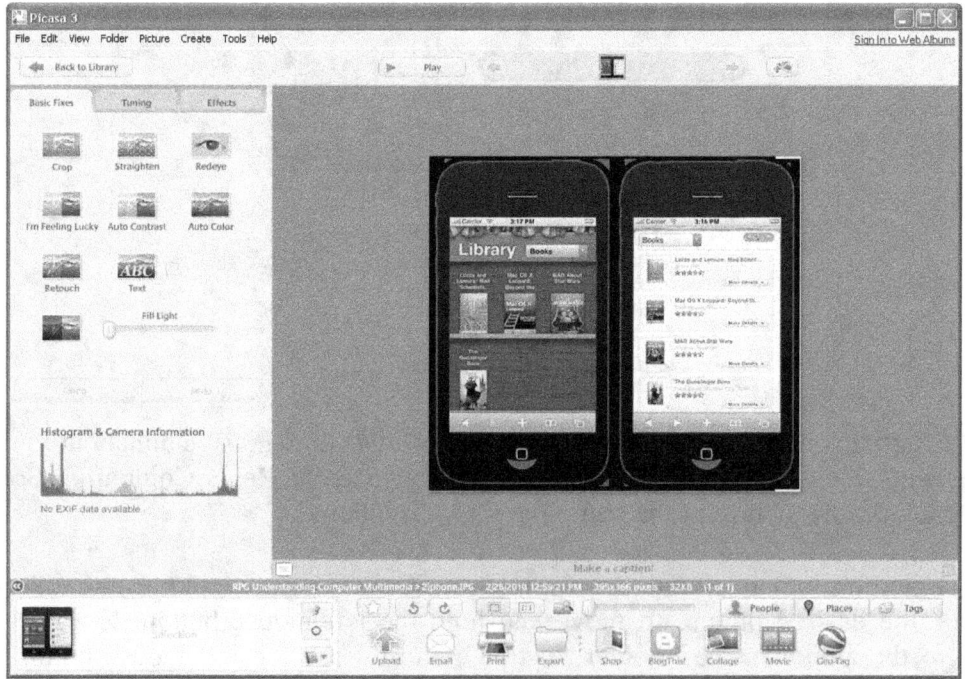

On the left side of the screen, you notice the "Basic Fixes" menu as shown in the picture below on the left. One of the options on this menu is the Crop option. Single left click the Crop menu option, and the crop photo menu will come up as shown in the picture below on the right.

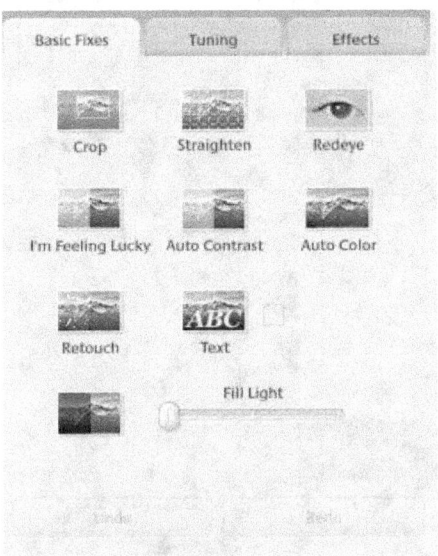

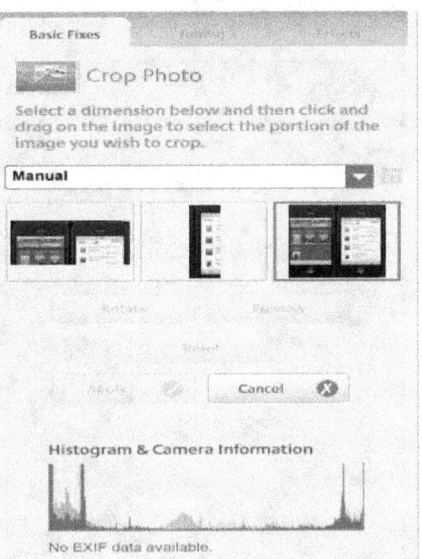

Basic Fixes Menu   Crop Photo Menu

To actually crop a picture, move your mouse cursor to the top left section of the part of the picture you want to crop, then single left click the left mouse button and hold it down. Drag your mouse to the bottom-right of the picture you want to crop and let go of the left mouse button. The section you want to crop should be highlighted, and the item that will be removed will be shaded out as shown in the picture below:

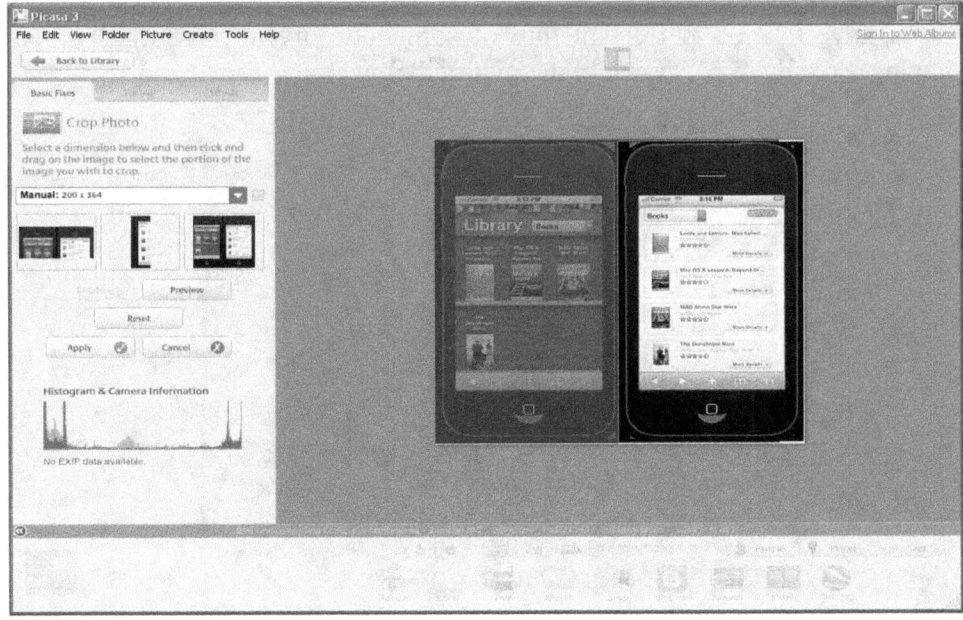

Then single left click the "Apply" button on the crop menu to crop the picture. It should look like the picture shown below. You have now successfully cropped your picture. Single left click the "Back To Library" button to go back to the main menu.

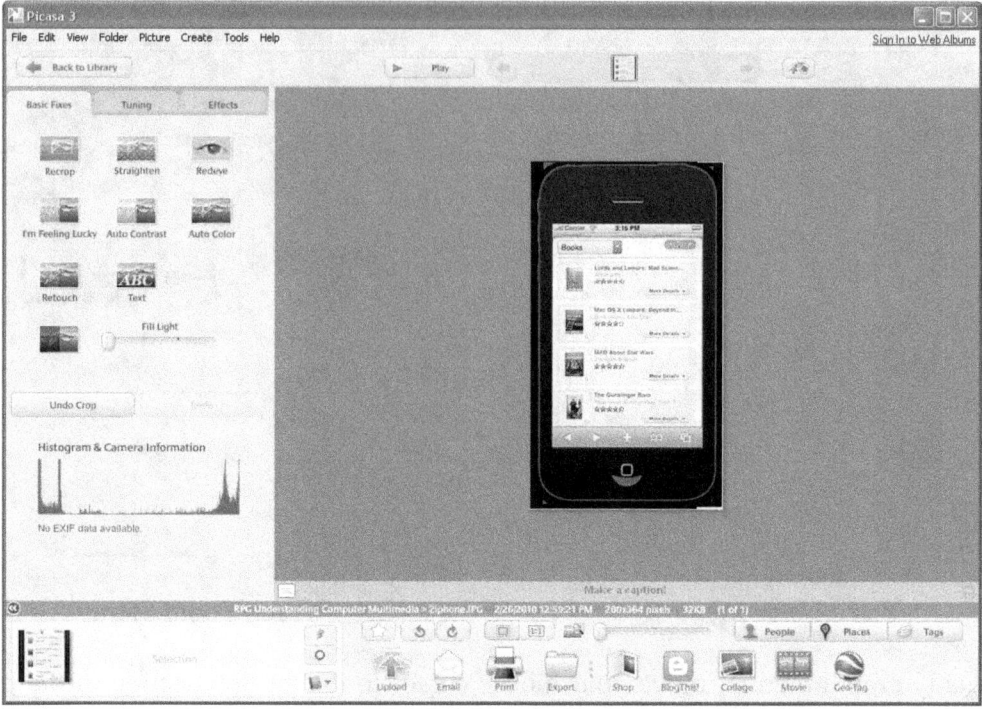

How To Correct Red Eye In Pictures

What if you have taken a perfect picture of someone only to have that person in the picture having a red eye? As shown in the picture below:

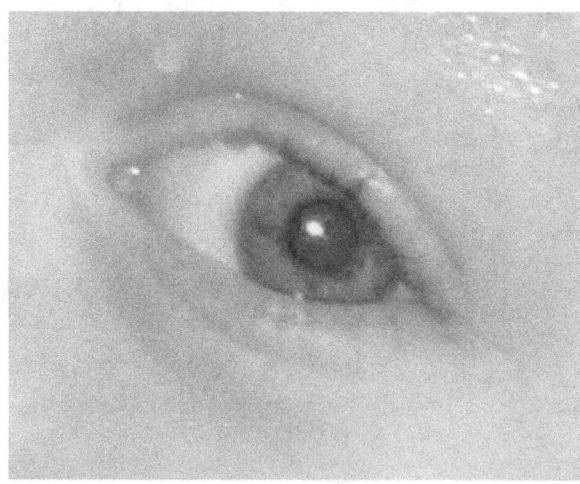

Picasa allows you to correct red eye in pictures. To correct red eye in Picasa, first open up the Picasa Program and find the picture that you want to correct. Double left click to open the picture. Your screen should look like the picture shown below:

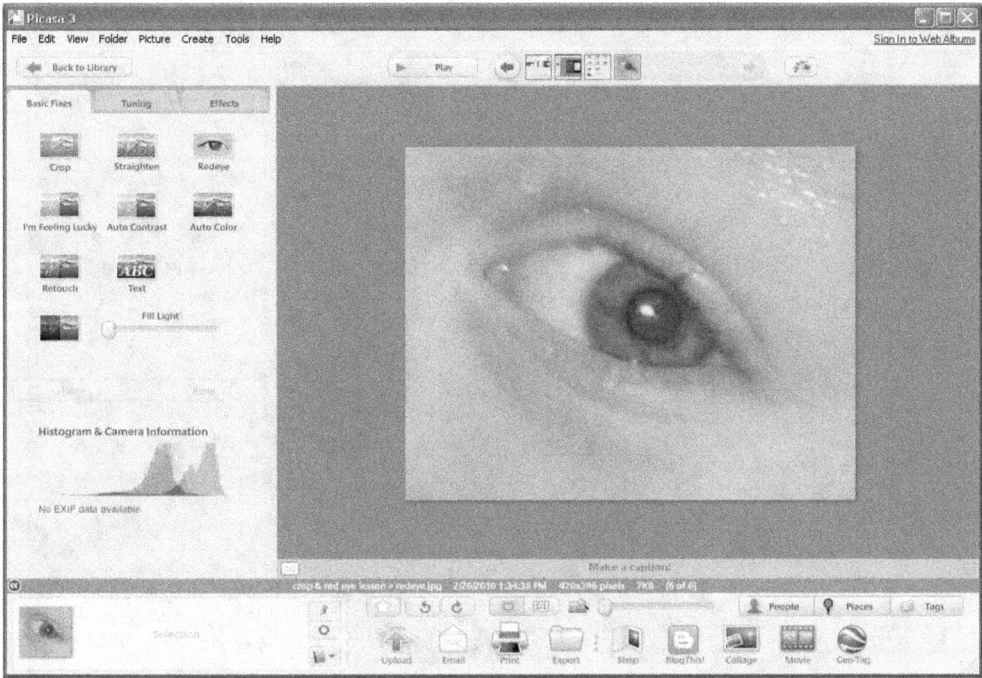

On the left side of the screen, you notice the "Basic Fixes" menu as shown in the picture below on the left. One of the options in this menu is the Red eye option. Single left click the Red eye option, and the Red eye menu will come up as shown in the picture below on the right.

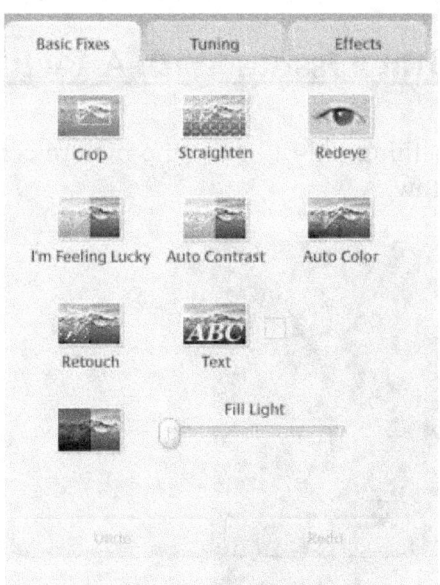

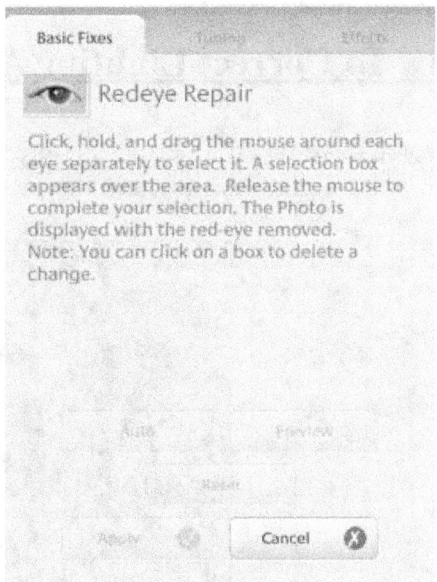

Basic Fixes Menu   Red Eye Menu

To remove red eye in a picture, move your mouse cursor to the top left section of the eye. Single left click the left mouse button and hold it down. Drag your mouse to the bottom-right section of the eye you want to correct and let go of the left mouse button. The eye you want to correct should be highlighted as shown in the picture below:

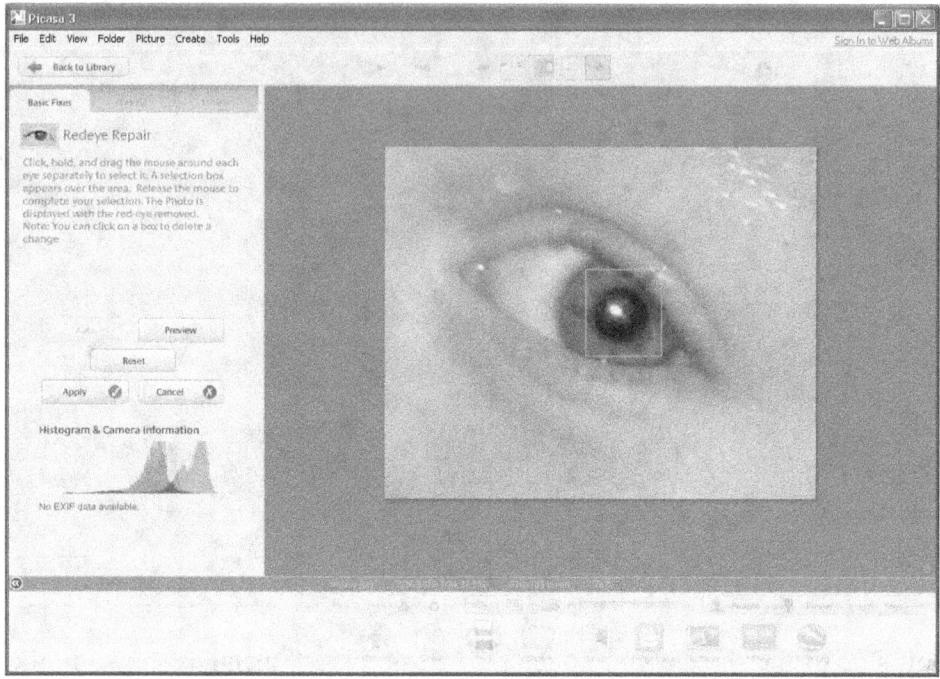

Single left click the "Apply" button on the Red eye menu to correct the picture. You have now successfully fixed the red eye in your picture. Single left click the "Back To Library" button to go back to the main menu.

How To Correct Lighting And Other Issues With A Picture

What if you have taken a perfect picture of something only to have the picture come out too dark or too light? As shown in the picture below:

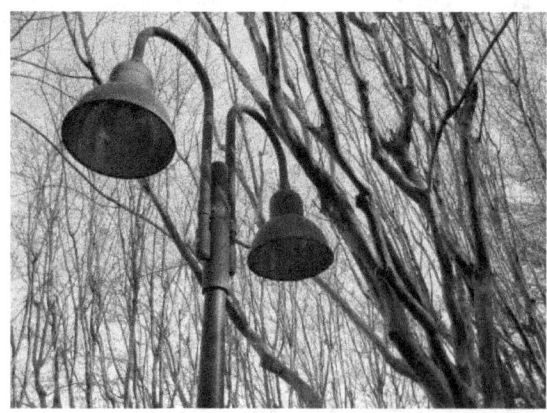

Picasa allows you to correct lighting and other problems in pictures. To correct pictures in Picasa, first open up the Picasa Program and find the picture that you want to correct and double left click the picture to open it. Your screen should look like the picture shown below:

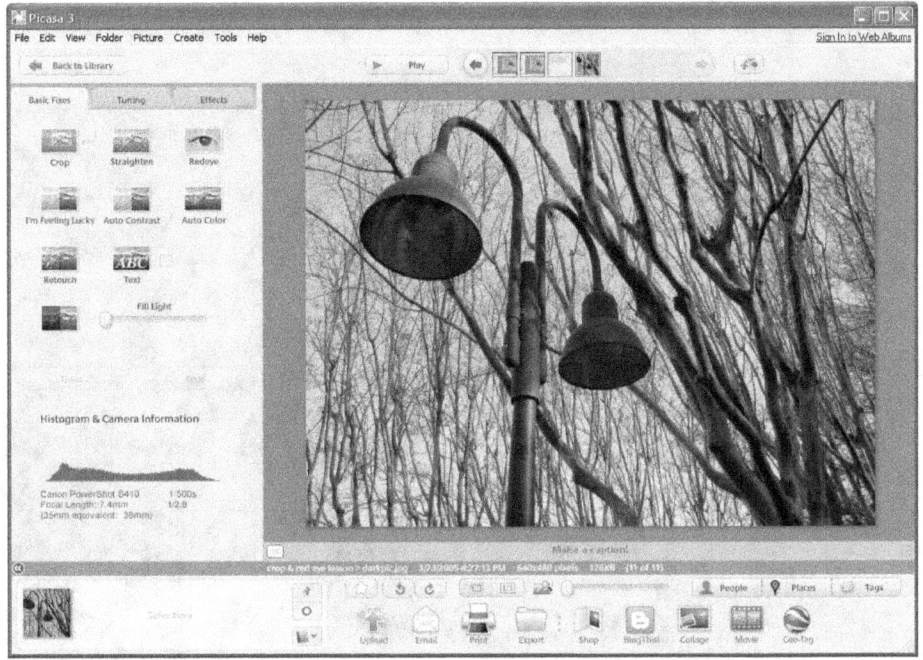

On the left side of the screen, you notice the "Basic Fixes" menu as shown in the picture below. One of the options in this menu is the "I'm Feeling Lucky" option. Single left click the I'm Feeling Lucky menu.

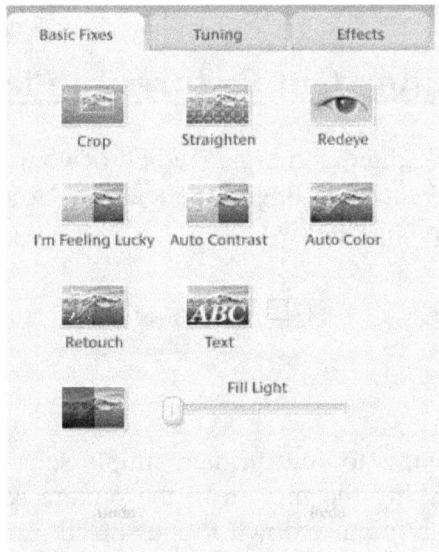

Basic Fixes Menu

When you single left click the "I'm Feeling Lucky" menu Item, Picasa then auto-corrects the lighting, sharpness and other issues with that particular picture. In the case of this particular picture, the picture was too light, so Picasa autocorrects the picture for e-mailing, printing and other things.

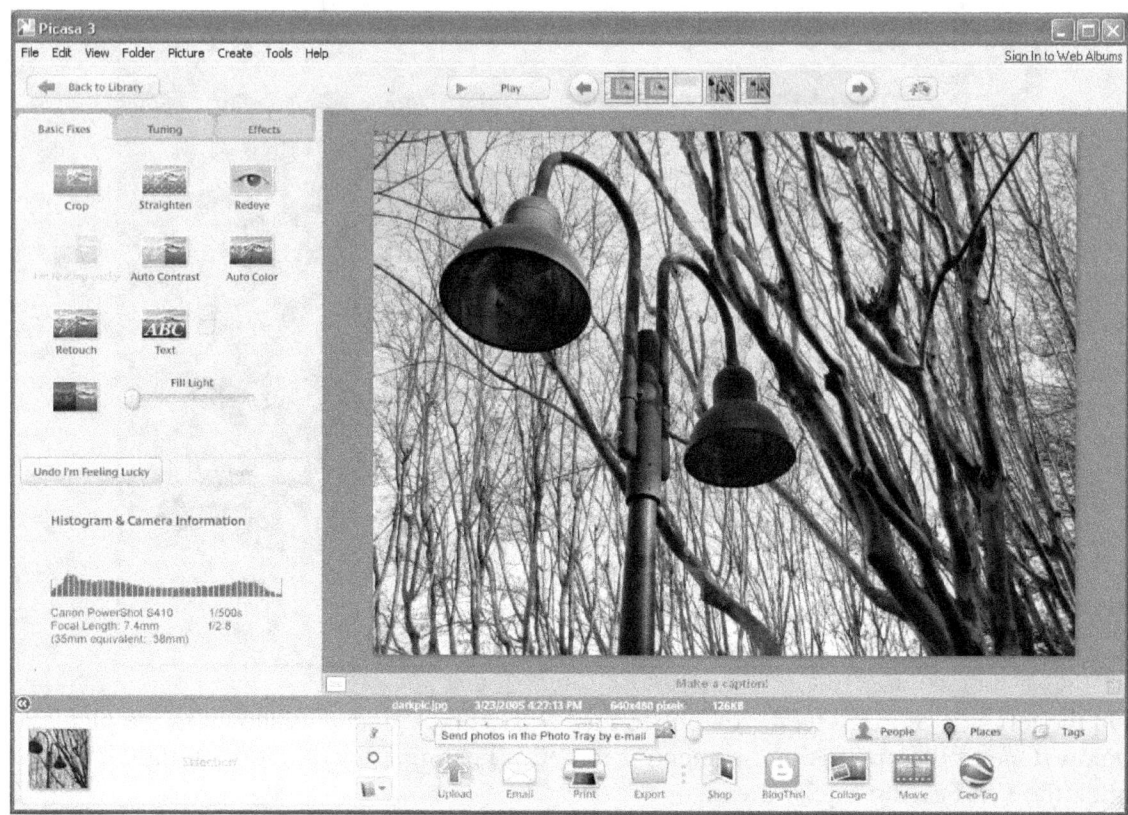

Printing Out Pictures In Picasa

After you have downloaded, edited and organized all of your pictures, you want to easily share them right? That leads me to telling you about the "Actions Section" of the Picasa main window shown in the picture below:

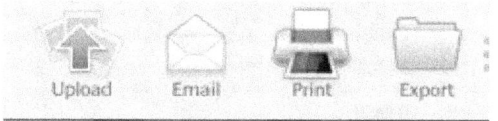

To print pictures in your albums to your printer, simply select one of your pictures from an album by single left clicking the picture in the picture section, and holding the left mouse button down. Drag the picture down to the selection tray in the action section of the main window and let go of the left button on your mouse. It looks like the picture shown on the next page:

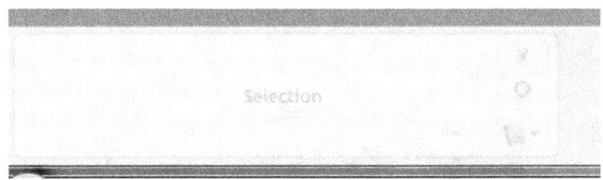

When you let go of your mouse button, your picture should then appear in this window with a green circle on the photo looking like the picture below:

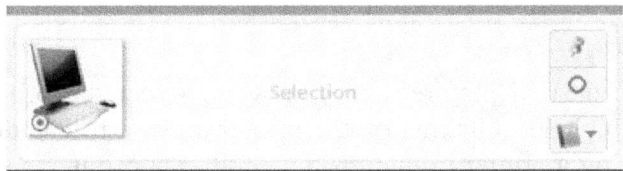

This will let you know that the picture was successfully inserted into the selection tray. Then go through the rest of your albums and select other pictures you wish to print and put them into the selection tray the same way. When you are done selecting pictures and want to print them, single left click the print button on the actions section. The print menu will come up looking like the picture shown below:

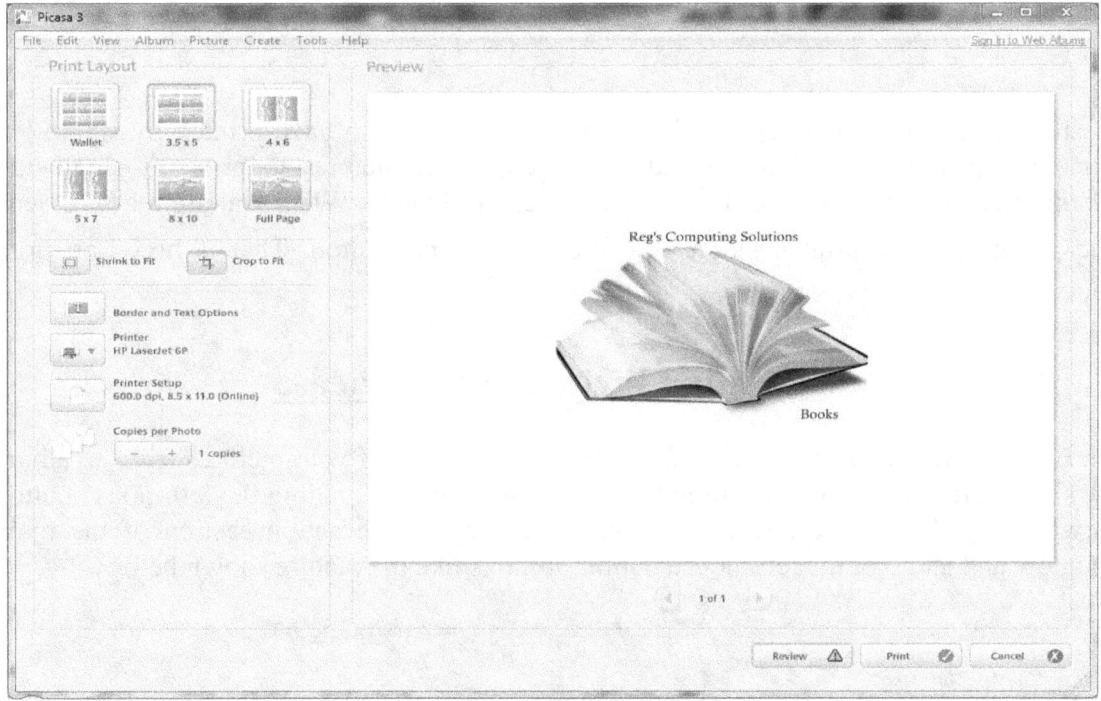

In this section, select the size of the picture that you want to print by single left clicking on desired size on the top left part of the layout menu that looks like the picture on the next page:

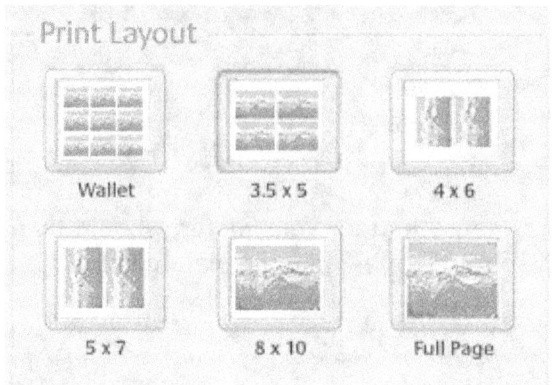

After you select the desired picture size you want, select the printer you want these pictures printed by single left clicking on the printer down arrow under the printer menu, then single left click on a printer in that drop menu to choose it. As shown in the picture below:

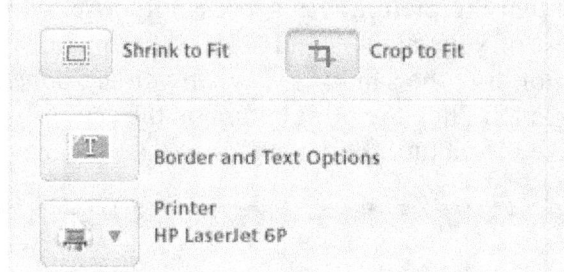

Lastly, select how many copies of each picture you wish to have printed by single left clicking the plus symbol to add additional copies of pictures to print, or single left clicking the minus symbol to print fewer copies of pictures. When you are ready to send the pictures to the printer, single left click the "Print" button. That is how you print pictures from Picasa.

E-Mailing Pictures From Picasa

To E-Mail pictures in your albums from Picasa, select one of your pictures from an album by single left clicking the picture in the picture section, and holding the left mouse button down. Drag the picture down to the selection tray in the action section of the main window and let go of the left mouse button. It looks like the picture shown below:

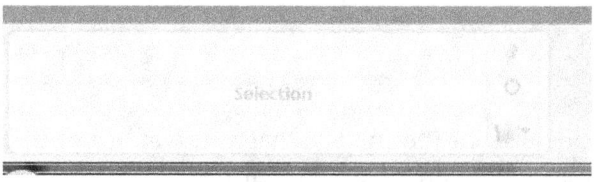

When you let go of your mouse button, your picture should then appear in this window with a green circle on the photo looking like the picture below:

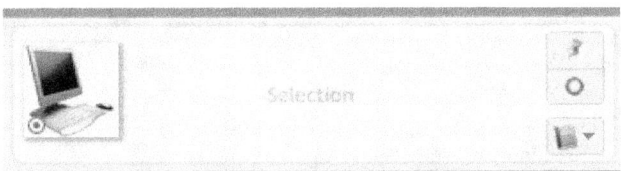

This will let you know that the picture was successfully inserted into the selection tray. Then go through the rest of your albums, select other pictures you wish to email and put them into the selection tray the same way. When you are done selecting pictures and want to email them, single left click the E-Mail button on the actions section. The E-Mail menu will come up looking like the picture shown below:

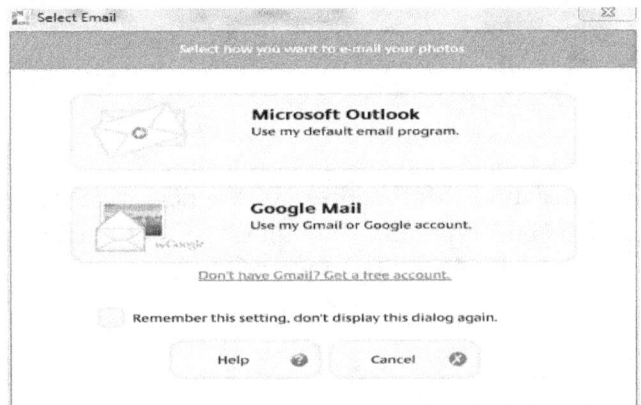

If you have Outlook installed and working on your computer, single left click the Microsoft Outlook button. Microsoft Outlook will then open up a new mail message with the selected pictures attached to this message. All you have to do is enter the E-Mail address of the person this message is going to, the subject of the E-Mail, type out your message and single left click the "Send" button. Your selected pictures are now E-Mailed from Picasa.

If you have a Google Gmail E-Mail account, single left click the Google Mail button. Sign into Gmail and Picasa will then open up a new mail message with the selected pictures attached to this message as shown in the picture on the next page:

Note – Picasa at this time does not support any other e-mail programs or online e-mail services such as Yahoo mail or Hotmail.

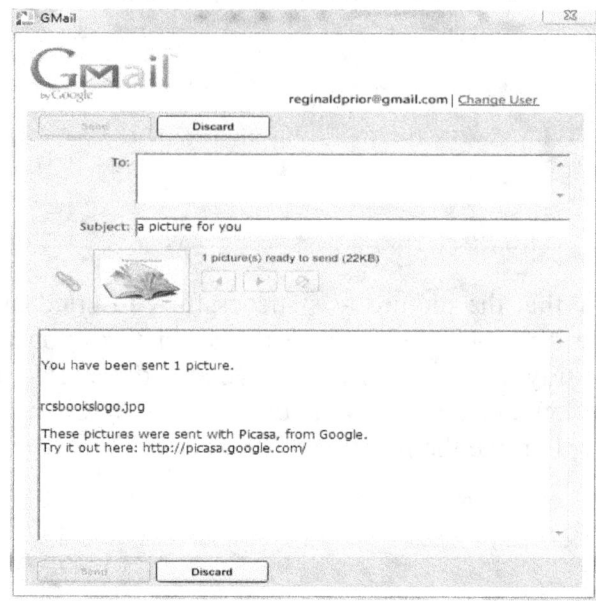

All you have to do is enter the E-Mail address of the person these pictures are going to, the subject of the E-Mail, and type out your message and single left click the "Send" button. Your pictures are now E-Mailed from your Gmail account from Picasa.

Using Windows Media Player to Download And Organize Music

Most people have a collection of music CD's in their houses and cars. It is also a known fact that these CD's can easily be scratched and damaged by even light use. You can backup music from your CD's and still enjoy them without scratching them by using Windows Media Player. With Windows Media Player, you can download music from your CD's to your computer, create playlists of your favorite songs and transfer them to a MP3 Player, CD or an Apple IPod for enjoyment on the go. I will explain how to do that and more in the upcoming sections.

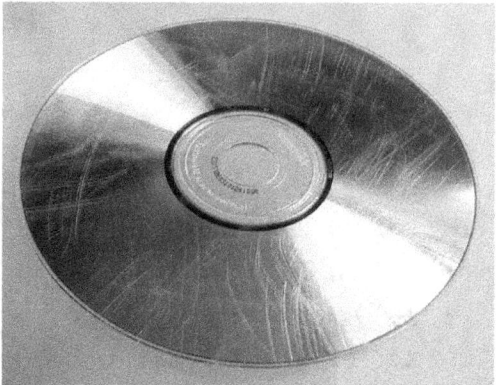
Picture of a Scratched CD

To get to Windows Media Player, move your mouse cursor to the start menu and single left click on it. The start menu will come up as shown in the picture below:

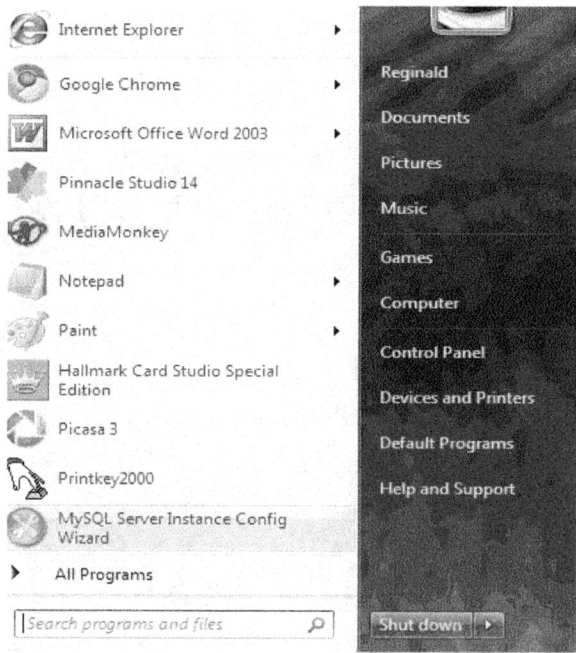

Single left click the "All Programs" link and single left click the "Windows Media Player Icon" which looks like the icon on the next page:

Windows Media Player will then start and look like the picture below:

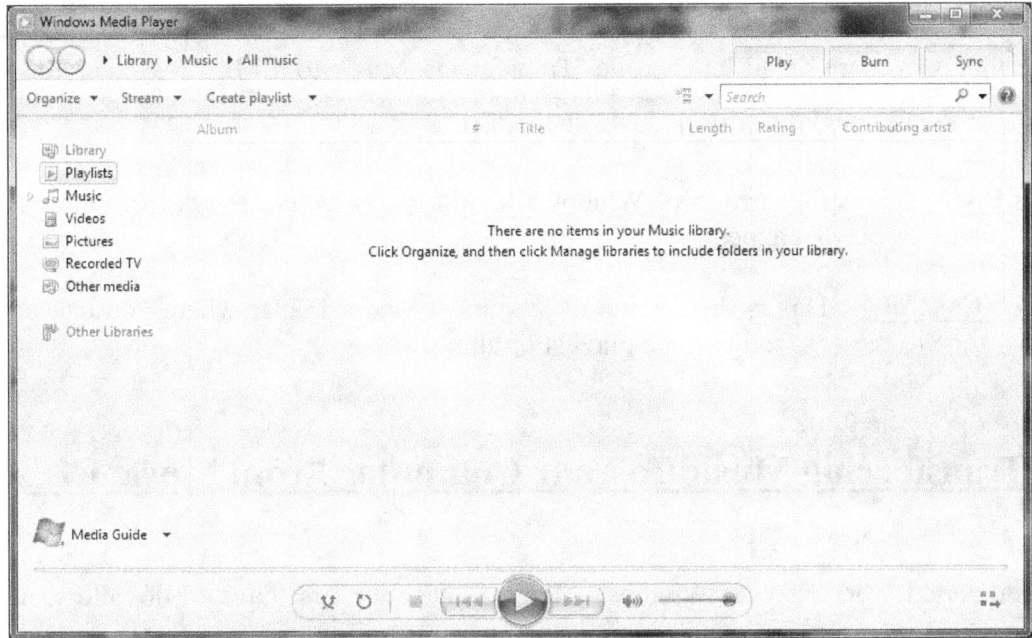

As you can see in the picture below, Windows Media Player has four separate sections.

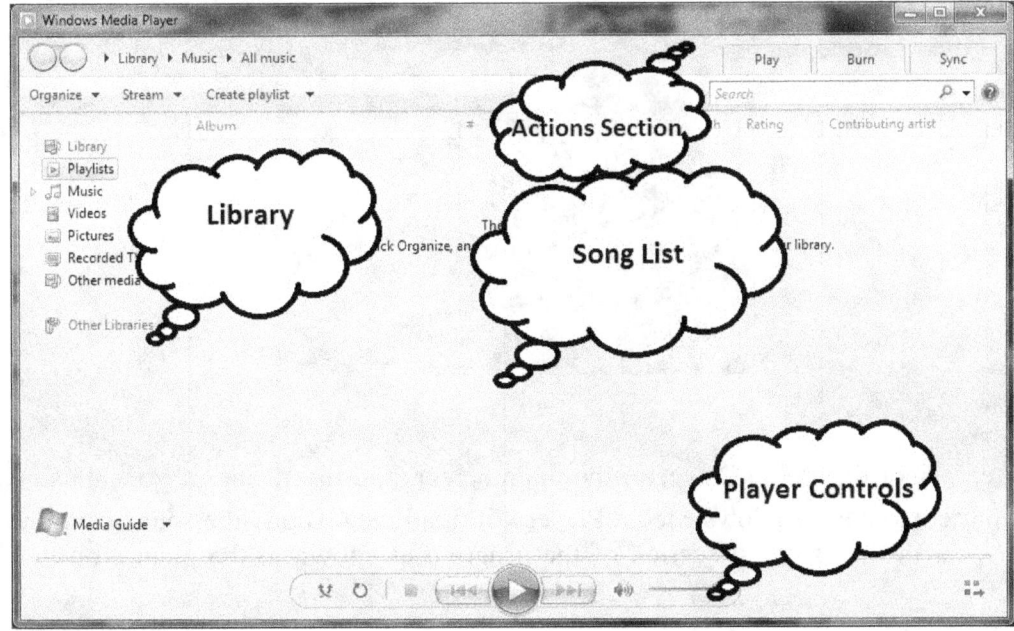

The four sections and what functions they provide with Windows Media Player are as follows:

Library – The Library is the part of Windows Media Player where you can quickly find and sort all of your music files.

Actions Section – This is the part of Windows Media Player where you could burn music CD's and download music to a MP3 player or an Apple IPod. We will discuss both of these things in more detail later in the "Transferring Music to a MP3 Player or IPod for Music on the Go" and the "Burning Music to CD's" sections.

Song List - This is the section of Windows Media Player where songs from the current artist, album or playlist appear.

Player Controls – This is the section of Windows Media Player where you can pause, replay or go to the next song on the playlist or album.

Transferring Music To Your Computer From Music CD's

To get started working with Windows Media Player, we first have to download music from your music CD's to your computer. And to do that, get your favorite music CD's together to import into your computer.

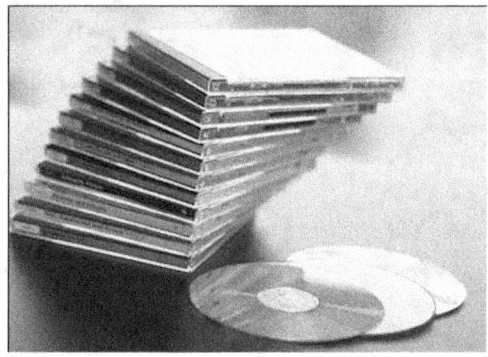

Open up Windows Media Player to the main screen and insert one of your music CD's into your computer. Windows Media Player will read the CD and the songs from the CD will appear in the song list section of the program as shown in the picture on the next page:

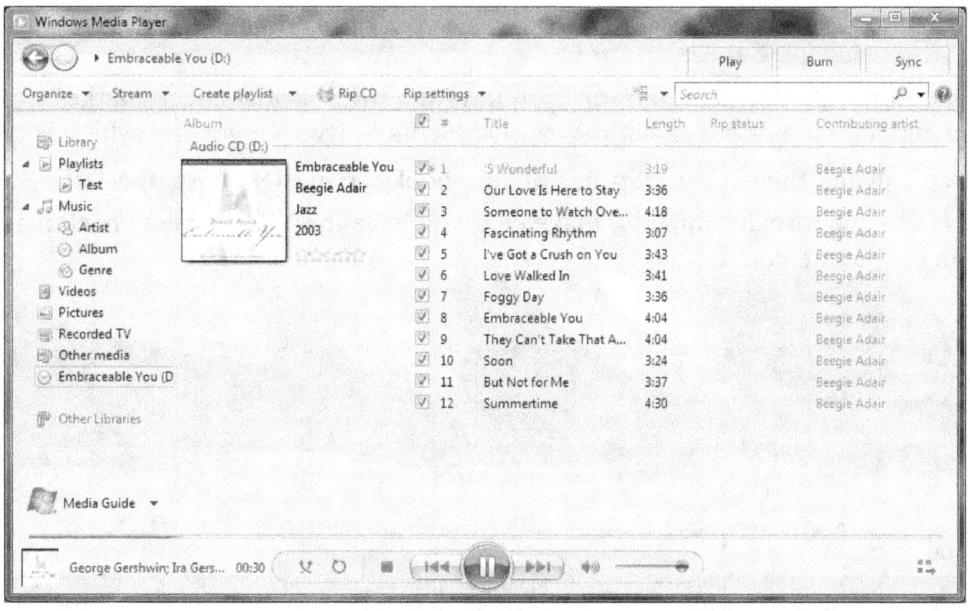

The next step to transferring a music CD to your computer is first making sure that Windows Media Player transfers the music to your computer into the MP3 format. This format is most compatible with just about every MP3 player or Apple IPod.

And to do that, depends on which version of Windows Media Player you have installed on your computer. In Windows Media Player 11, which is installed for Windows XP and Vista, move your mouse cursor to the down arrow under the "Rip" button and single left click on it. A submenu will show up as shown in the picture below.

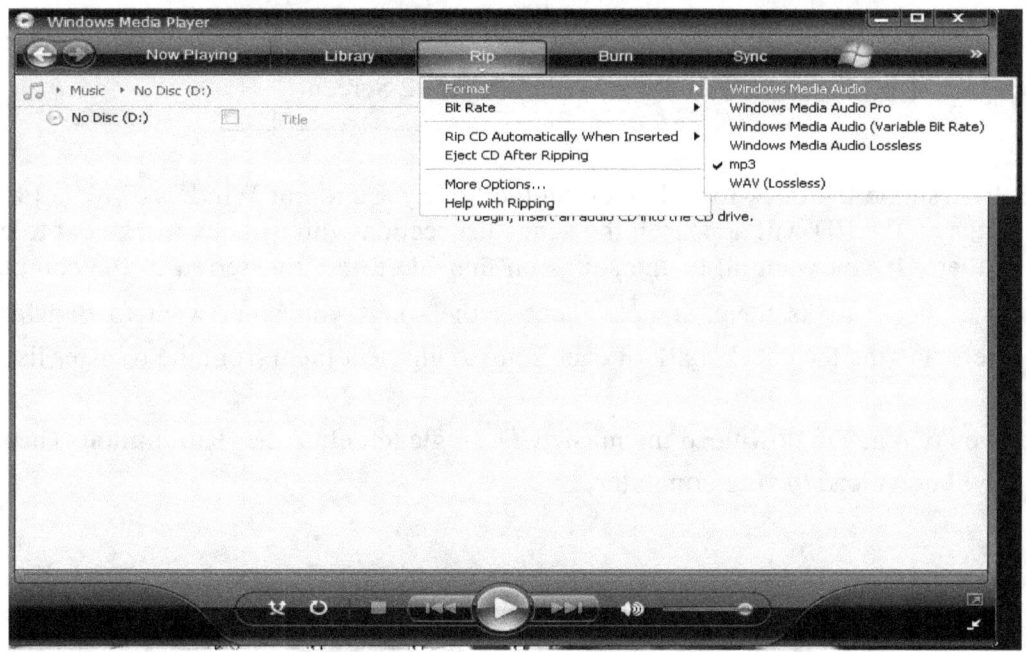

Windows Media Player 11 Screen

Under the format submenu, make sure you have the MP3 format check marked as shown in the picture on the last page. With Windows Media Player Version 12, which is only for Windows 7 at the time of the writing of this book, single left click the "Rip Settings" button. Under the format submenu, make sure you have the MP3 format check marked as shown in the picture below.

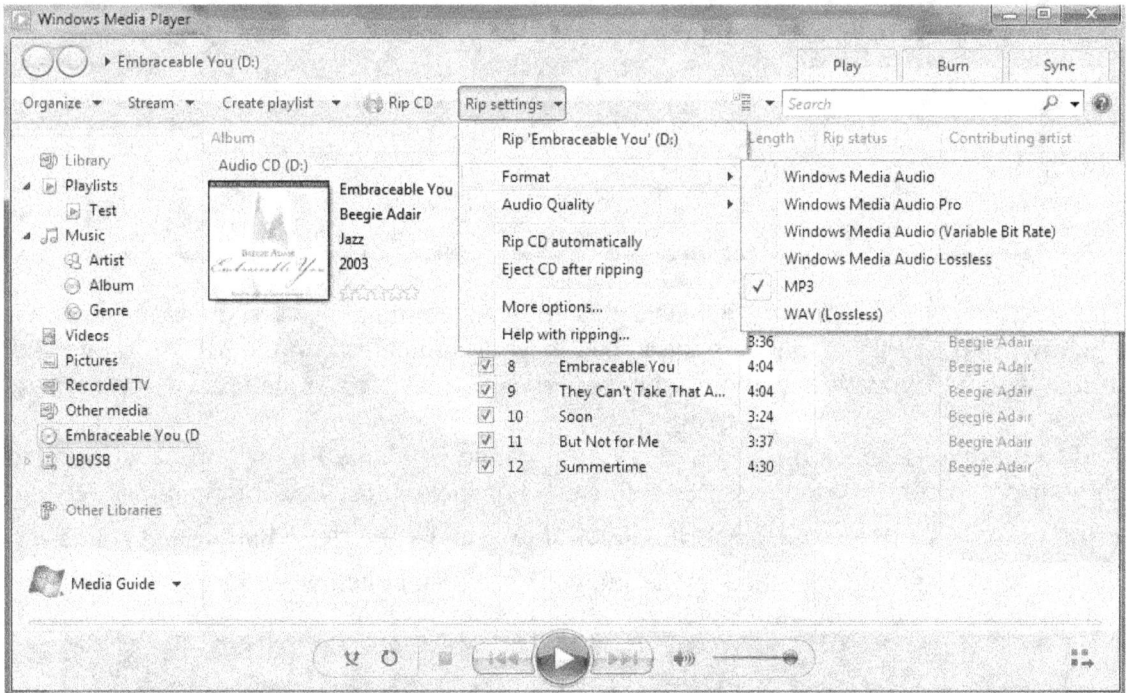

Windows Media Player 12 Screen

After that, single left click the CD icon on the library section of Windows Media Player. The songs on the CD will appear in the songs list section with a check mark next to each one of them. If you want all of the songs on this CD to be transferred to the computer, leave the check marks there. If not, uncheck the songs you don't want to transfer by single left clicking the check mark of each song to unselect them from the transfer list.

When you're ready to download the music CD, single left click the "Rip" button. Then the music will download to your computer.

Creating Music Playlists

Remember when you could make a cassette tape of all of your favorite songs from other cassette tapes? You can still do that with your digital music collection by using playlists. To create a playlist, on the main screen of Windows Media Player, move your mouse cursor and single left click the "Create Playlist" button.

When you do this, in the library section under the playlist section, an icon will show up with "Untitled Playlist" highlighted as shown in the picture below. Type in a new name for the playlist and press the enter key on your keyboard. This will name this particular playlist.

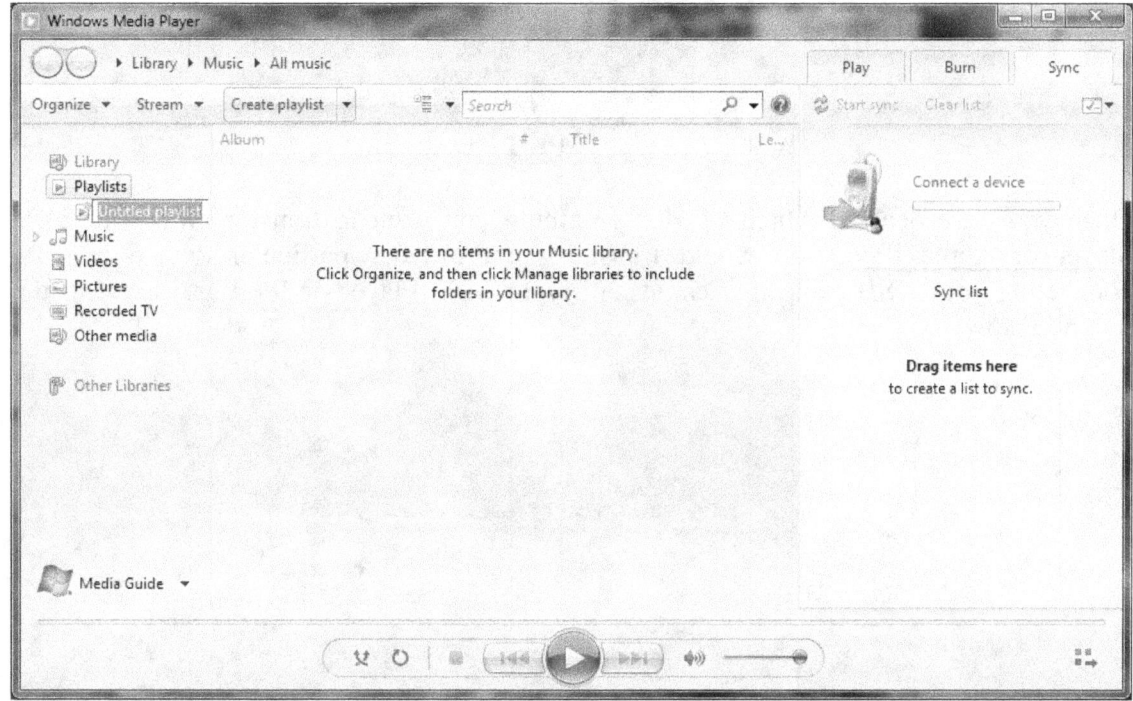

To add a song to this playlist you have just created, single left click the "Music" or "Artist" link in the library section. Your music collection will show up in the song list. Scroll down your music collection and when you see a particular song that you want to add, single left click and hold the left mouse button down on the song. Drag the song over to the actual playlist icon in the library section and let go of the left mouse button.

For each song you want to add to this or any other playlist, repeat the previous step until you have all of the songs you want in the playlist. From this playlist, you can burn a CD of it, or upload to an MP3 Player or an Apple IPod for enjoyment on the go. I will go over both of these options in the upcoming sections.

Transferring Music To A MP3 Player Or IPod For Music On The Go

One of the features of Windows Media Player is the option of being able to transfer your music from your computer to a MP3 Player or Apple IPod. These devices allow you to enjoy your music without having to have your music CD's at all. These devices can hold quite a bit of music on them depending on the size of your particular player.

For example, a 2GB MP3 player or Apple IPod can hold about 300 songs. That is about the equivalent of eleven CD's of music!

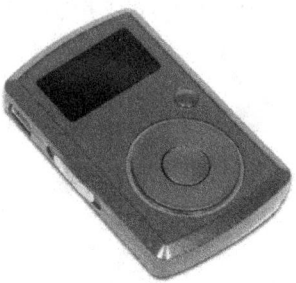

Once you have decided which playlist or album you want to transfer onto your MP3 player or Apple IPod, you would transfer them to your particular device by first connecting your USB cable that came with your MP3 Player or IPod as shown in the picture below:

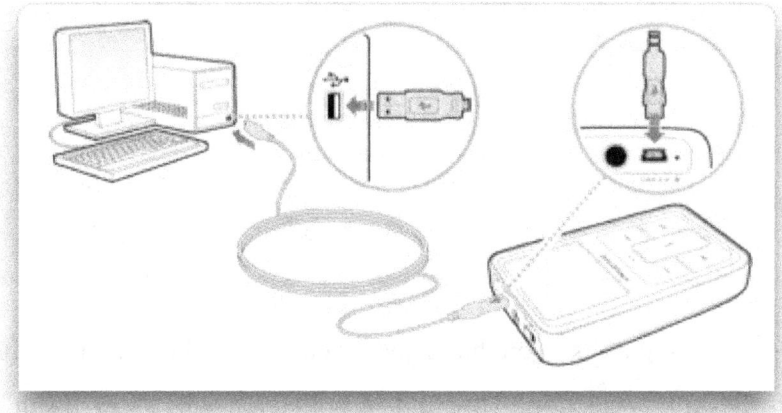

Your computer will then recognize your device and pop up a prompt menu for your device. Single left click the "X" button at the top of this prompt. Open up Windows Media Player and on the main screen, single left click the "Sync" tab. Your screen should look like the picture shown on the next page:

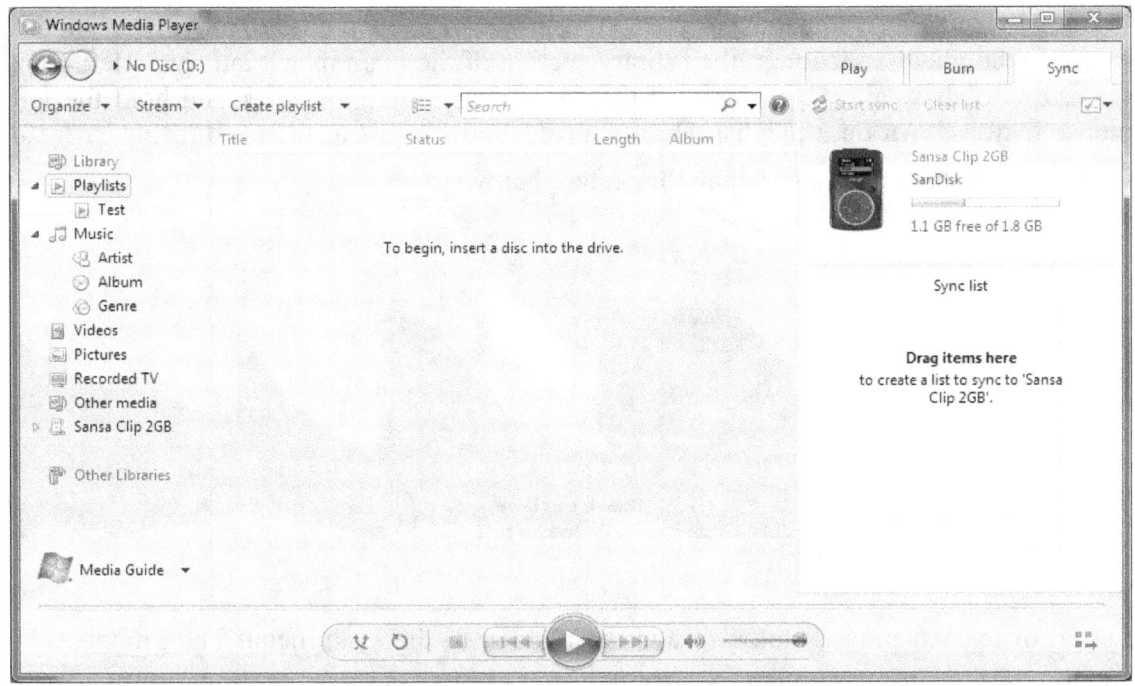

In this case, I have my SanDisk Sansa Clip connected to my computer. To actually transfer music from your computer to your MP3 Player or Apple IPod, first single left click the arrow next to the music menu in the Library section on the main menu. A submenu will come up with three choices, Artist, Album & Genre. Single left click on Artist.

All of the music that you have downloaded onto your computer will come up in the song list section, arranged by Artist. Double left click an artist to show songs and individual albums you have from that artist on your computer. To transfer an individual song to your MP3 Player or Apple IPod, move your mouse cursor to the song and single left click and hold the left mouse button down. Drag the song to the sync list where it says "Drag Items Here" and let go of the left mouse button. Repeat for each song you want to transfer. Then move your mouse cursor to the "Start Sync" button and single left click on it to transfer to your MP3 Player or Apple IPod.

To transfer a complete album, move your mouse cursor to the album cover and single left click and hold the left mouse button down. Drag the album cover to the sync list and let go of the left mouse button. Repeat for each album you want to transfer. Then move your mouse cursor to the "Start Sync" button and single left click on it to transfer to your MP3 Player or Apple IPod.

If you want to transfer a playlist to your MP3 Player or an Apple IPod, move your mouse cursor to the playlist section in the Library section of the main menu and single left click the arrow to show all of your created playlists. Then single left click and hold the left mouse button down on a playlist. Drag your desired playlist to the sync menu where it says "Drag Items Here" as shown in the picture below:

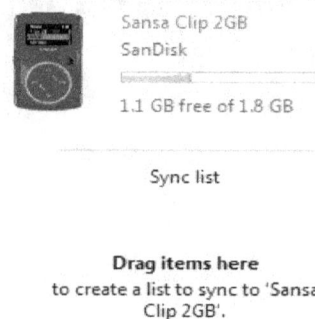

Sync list

Drag items here
to create a list to sync to 'Sansa Clip 2GB'.

Let go of the left mouse button to add the playlist to the sync menu. Then move your mouse cursor to the "Start Sync" button and single left click on it to transfer to your MP3 Player or Apple IPod.

Enjoying Music On Your MP3 Player In Your Car

Once you have loaded your MP3 Player with your favorite songs, you want to play them in your car on the way to work or doing other errands right? Well if your car has a cassette player installed in it, buy a cassette adapter. You usually can find these at Wal-Mart or Best Buy in the electronics section. It looks like the picture shown below:

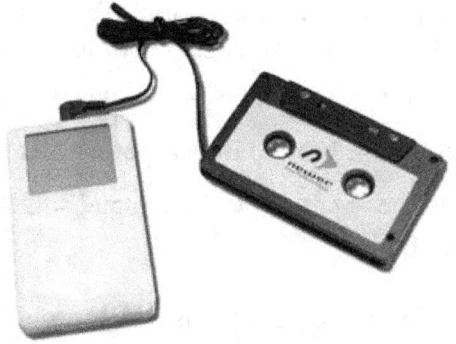

Cassette Tape Adapter

As shown in the picture above, it looks like a cassette tape with a cable coming out of it. The cable coming out of it is a headphone adapter that plugs into the headphone jack of your MP3 player or Apple IPod. You will insert the cassette into your car radio's cassette deck and then operate your MP3 player or Apple IPod to play the music through your car speakers.

If you have a car that was made within the last 10 years and it does not have a cassette player, you can still enjoy your music on your MP3 Player or Apple IPod in your car. To do that, buy what is called a FM Transmitter. You usually can find these at Wal-Mart or Best Buy in the electronics section. It looks like the picture shown on the below:

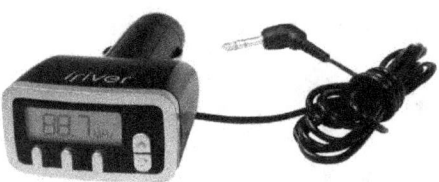

FM Modulator

What this device does is that it plugs into your cigarette lighter for power and shows a radio station as shown in the picture above. You will plug the other cable into your MP3 Players headphone jack. Then tune your car radio to the radio station that shows on the FM modulator. Then operate your MP3 player or Apple IPod to play the music through your car speakers.

With an FM Modulator, sometimes the initial radio frequency that is programmed in when you first buy and install it may have a lot of static. In that case, you will have to tune the FM Modulator to another frequency that has a less staticky sound. For your particular FM Modulator, you will have to refer to the user manual for instructions on how to change the radio station frequency.

NOTE – When going to purchase an FM Modulator, please keep in mind that they are two models of FM Modulators. One of them is only for an Apple IPod and the other kind are for any other MP3 Player.

Burning Music To CD's

If you don't have an MP3 player or Apple IPod at your disposal and want to burn music CD's, Windows Media Player allows you to do that also. To burn albums or playlists to blank CD's, move your mouse cursor on the Windows Media Player main menu and single left click the "Burn" button. Your screen should look like the picture shown below:

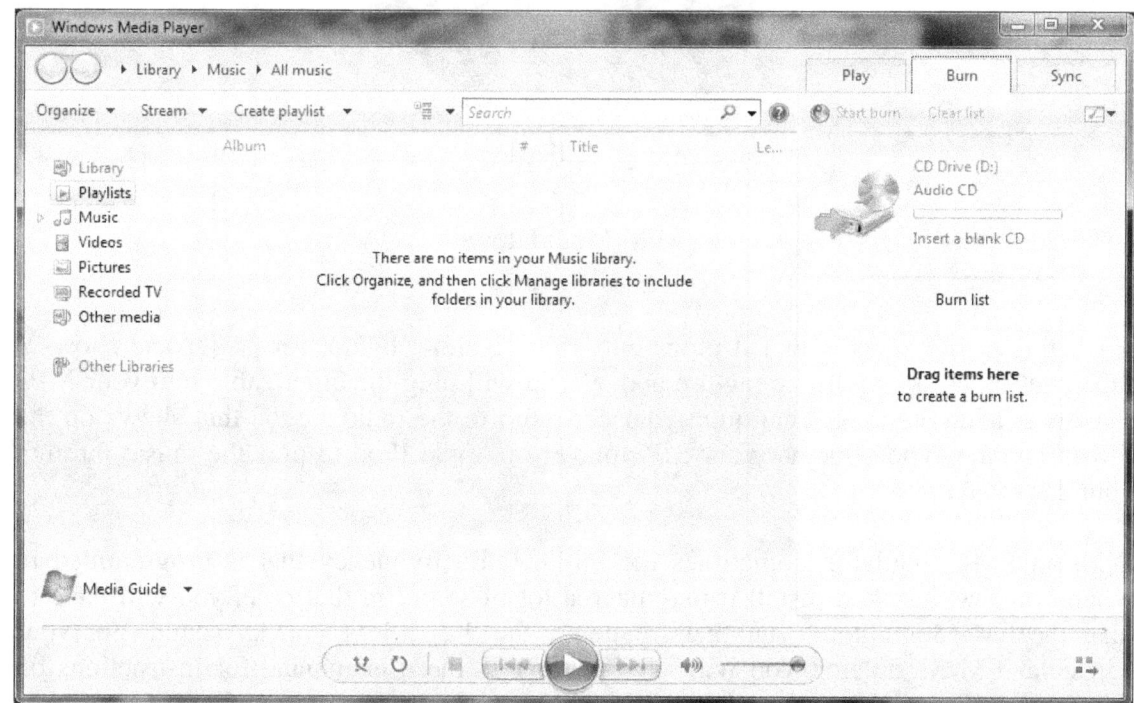

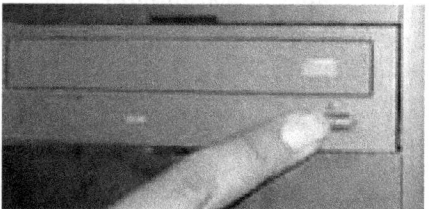

Insert a blank CD into your CD burner. Move your mouse cursor and single left click the arrow next to the music menu in the Library section on the main menu. A submenu will come up with three choices, Artist, Album & Genre. Single left click on Artist.

All of the music that you have downloaded onto your computer will come up in the song list section, arranged by Artist. Double left click an artist to show songs and individual albums you have from that artist on your computer. To transfer an individual song to your blank CD, move your mouse cursor to the song and single left click and hold the left mouse button. Drag the song to the burn list where it says "Drag Items Here" and let go of the left mouse button. Repeat for each song you want to transfer.

To transfer a complete album, move your mouse cursor to the album cover, single left click and hold the left mouse button down. Drag the album cover to the burn list and let go of the left mouse button. Repeat for each album you want to transfer. If you want to transfer a playlist to your blank CD, move your mouse cursor to the playlist section in the Library section of the main menu and single left click the arrow to show all of your created playlists.

Single left click and hold the left mouse button down on a playlist. Drag your desired playlist to the burn menu where it says "Drag Items Here" as shown in the picture below, and let go of the left mouse button to add the playlist.

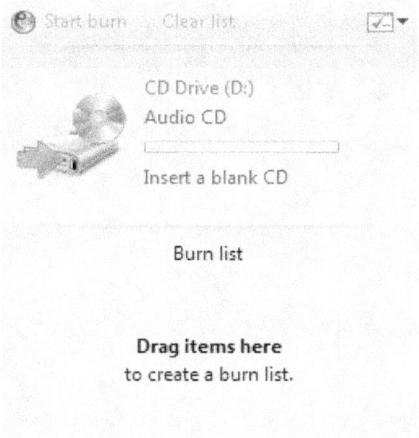

When you are ready to create your custom CD, then move your mouse cursor to the "Start Burn" button and single left click on it to burn that playlist to your blank CD.

I hope that you have gained a lot of knowledge in learning more about how to download and work with your pictures and music by reading this book. Just like in the preface, you are the most important critic and value all of your feedback about this book so that I can improve future texts. Thank you for reading and look forward to hearing from you!!

Reginald T. Prior

www.ingramcontent.com/pod-product-compliance
Lightning Source LLC
Chambersburg PA
CBHW081230170526
45165CB00009B/3026